Mr. Pim Passes By

Alan Alexander Milne

Contents

ACT I 7

ACT II 48

ACT III 82

PROPERTY PLOT 116

   ACT I 116

   ACT II 121

   ACT III 122

MR. PIM PASSES BY

BY

Alan Alexander Milne

ACT I

The morning-room at Marden House (Buckinghamshire) decided more than a hundred years ago that it was all right, and has not bothered about itself since. Visitors to the house have called the result such different adjectives as "mellow," "old-fashioned," "charming"--even "baronial" and "antique;" but nobody ever said it was "exciting." Sometimes OLIVIA wants it to be more exciting, and last week she rather let herself go over some new curtains; she still has the rings to put on. It is obvious that the curtains alone will overdo the excitement; they will have to be harmonized with a new carpet and cushions. *OLIVIA* has her eye on just the things, but one has to go carefully with *GEORGE.* What was good enough, for his great-great-grandfather is good enough for him. However, we can trust *OLIVIA* to see him through it, although it may take time.

A scene plot is given at the end of the play.

There are three ways of coming into the room: by the open windows leading from the garden, by the doors to R., or by the staircase from up R, MR. PIM *chooses the latter way--or rather* ANNE chooses it for him; and *MR. PIM* kindly and inoffensively follows her. She comes down steps and crosses to *C.,* followed by MR. PIM.

ANNE (*moves up, looking off* L. *and returning to* PIM R.C.). I'll tell Mr. Marden you're here, sir. Mr. Pim, isn't it?

PIM (*nervously*). Yes--er--Mr. Pim--Mr. Carraway Pim. He doesn't know me, you understand, but if he could just spare me a few moments--er--- (*He fumbles in his pockets*.) I gave you that letter?

ANNE. Yes, sir, I'll give it to him.

PIM (brings out a stamped letter which is not the one he was looking for, but which reminds him of something else he has forgotten. Looking at letter). Oh! Dear me!

ANNE. Yes, sir?

PIM. Dear me. I ought to have posted this. (*Looking at letter*.) Oh, well, I must send a telegram. You have a telegraph office in the village?

ANNE. Oh, yes, sir. (*Moving up to terrace up* L. *and pointing off* L.) If you turn to the left when you get outside the gates, it's about a hundred yards down the hill. Turn to the left and down the hill.

PIM. Turn to the left and down the hill. Thank you, thank you. Very stupid of me to have forgotten.

(ANNE *exits up staircase R*.)

(MR. PIM wanders about the room humming to himself, and looking at the pictures and photos on piano. Then goes out at window up L.) (DINAH *enters from staircase up* R. dancing, and humming the air of "Down on the Farm:" she is nineteen, very pretty, very happy, and full of boyish high spirits and conversation. She dances to foot of stairs, looks off R., *then down* C., then to piano; sits and plays a few bars and sings "Down on the Farm," rises and moves up to *R.* of piano, and as she does so *PIM* re-enters from window up *L.* and they come suddenly face to face up back *C.* below the writing-table. There is a slight pause.)

DINAH (*backing a step*). Hullo!

PIM. You must forgive me, but... Good morning, Mrs. Marden.

DINAH. Oh, I say, *I*'m not Mrs. Marden. I'm Dinah.

PIM (*with a smile*). Then I will say, Good morning. Miss Diana.

DINAH (*reproachfully*). Now, look here, if you and I are going to be friends, you mustn't do that. Dinah, *not* Diana. Do remember it, there's a good man, because I get so tired of correcting people. (*Moving down* C. *to* B.) Have you come to stay with us? (*Sits on settee* R.)

PIM (*following her down*). Well, no, Miss--er--Dinah.

DINAH (*nodding*). That's right. I can see I shan't have to speak to *you* again. Now tell me your name, and I bet you I get it right first time. And do sit down.

PIM (*crossing to* L. *and sitting on settee* L.). Thank you. My name is--er--Pim, Carraway Pim--

DINAH. Pim, that's easy.

PIM. And I have a letter of introduction to your father--

DINAH (*rising and crossing to* R. *of table* L.C. *and speaking across same*). Oh, no; now you're going wrong again, Mr. Pim. George isn't my father; he's my uncle. Uncle George--he doesn't like me calling him George. Olivia doesn't mind--I mean she doesn't mind being called Olivia, but George is rather touchy. (*Sitting on table, facing* PIM.) You see, he's been my guardian since I was about two, and then about five years ago he married a widow called Mrs. Telworthy.

PIM (*repeating*). Mrs. Telworthy.

DINAH. That's Olivia--so she became my Aunt Olivia, only she lets me drop the Aunt. (*Speaking very sharply*.) Get that?

PIM (*a little alarmed*). I--I think so, Miss Marden.

DINAH (*admiringly*). I say, you *are* quick, Mr. Pim. Well, if you take my advice, when you've finished your business with George, you will hang about a bit and see if you can't see Olivia. (*Rising and moving* C.) She's simply--(*feeling for the word*)--devastating. I don't wonder George fell in love with her.

(*Moving to above piano* R., *looking at photos, etc.*)

PIM (*rising and looking at his watch and coming* C.). It's only the merest matter of business--just a few words with your uncle--Perhaps I'd better...

DINAH (*looking at photo on top end of piano*). Well, you must please yourself, Mr. Pim. I'm just giving you a friendly word of advice. Naturally, I was awfully glad to get such a magnificent aunt. (Moving down to *L.* of piano and taking up and looking at photo of OLIVIA.) Because, after all, marriage *is* rather a toss up, isn't it?--

PIM (*taken aback*). Well, I don't, know, I haven't had any experience...

DINAH (*continuing*). And George might have gone off with anybody.

(*Moving to* PIM.) It's different on the stage, where guardians always marry their wards, but George couldn't marry *me* because I'm his niece. Mind you, I don't say that I should have had him, because, between ourselves, he's a little bit old-fashioned.

PIM. So he married--er--Mrs. Marden instead.

DINAH. Mrs. Telworthy--don't say you've forgotten already, just when you were getting so good at names. Mrs. Telworthy. (Moves to and sits on settee R.) You see, Olivia married the Telworthy man and went to Australia with him, and he drank himself to death in the bush, or wherever you drink yourself to death out there, and Olivia came home to England, and met my uncle, and he fell in love with her and proposed to her--(*rises and kneels on settee*)--and he came into my room that night-- I was about fourteen--and turned on the light and said, "Dinah, how would you like to have a beautiful aunt of your very own?" (PIM *laughs*.) And I said: "Congratulations, George." (PIM *laughs again*.) That was the first time I called him George. Of course, I'd seen it coming for weeks. Telworthy, isn't it a funny name?

PIM. Oh, a most curious name--Telworthy. From Australia, you say?

DINAH. Yes, I always say that he's probably still alive, and will turn up here one morning and annoy George.

PIM (*shocked*). Oh!

DINAH. But I'm afraid there's not much chance.

PIM (*shocked*). Miss Marden! Really!

DINAH, Well, of course, I don't really *want* it to happen, but it *would* be rather exciting. (*Crossing to* PIM.) Wouldn't it, Mr Pim?

PIM. Exciting!

(PIM *crosses to below settee* L.)

DINAH. However, things like that never seem to occur down here, somehow, (*Running up into window up* R. PIM *watches her*.) There was a hayrick burnt last year about a mile away, but that isn't the same, is it?

PIM. No, I should say that that was certainly different.

DINAH (*coming to back of table* L.C.). Of course, something very, very wonderful did happen last night. (*Backing away*.) No, no! I'm not sure if I know you well enough--(*She looks at him hesitatingly*.)

PIM (*uncomfortably*). Really, Miss Marden, you mustn't. I am only a--a passer-by, here to-day and gone to-morrow. You really mustn't--

DINAH (*looking round and earning down to* PIM), And yet there's something about you, Mr. Pim, which inspires confidence.

PIM (*moving to* L.). Oh, no. Really, you mustn't tell me.

DINAH (*taking his arm*). The fact is--(*in a stage whisper*)--I got engaged last night!

PIM. Dear me, let me congratulate you. I wish somebody would come here.

DINAH (*running up to foot of staircase up* R. *and looking off*), I expect that's why George is keeping you such a long time. (*Turning to* PIM.) Brian, my young man, the well-known painter--only nobody has ever heard of him--he's smoking a pipe with George in the library and asking for his niece's hand. (*Coming back to* PIM, and taking his hands, she dances round with him in a circle.)

(PIM *falls exhausted and coughing on to settee* L. *and* DINAH laughing sits on settee R.)

DINAH. Isn't it exciting? You're really rather lucky, Mr. Pim--I mean being told so soon. Even Olivia doesn't know yet.

PIM. Yes, yes, I congratulate you, Miss Marden. Perhaps it would be better--(*About to get up*.)

(ANNE *comes in from staircase up* R. *She comes to* C.)

ANNE. Mr. Marden is out at the moment, sir--

DINAH (*disappointed*). Oh!

ANNE (*seeing* DINAH). Oh, I didn't see you, Miss Dinah!

PIM. Out! Eh? Dear! Dear!

DINAH, It's all right, Anne. (*Rising*.) *I'm* looking after Mr. Pim.

ANNE. Very well, Miss.

PIM (*sotto voce*). Out! Oh, well, I'd better go--

(*Exit* ANNE *up staircase* B.)

DINAH (*excitedy*). That's me. (Running up to foot of staircase and watching *ANNE* off.) They can't discuss me in the library without breaking down--(*coming down* R. *and imitating* GEORGE *and* BRIAN)--

so
they're walking up and down outside, and slashing at the thistles in
order to conceal their emotion. You know. I expect Brian--(Crossing up
to *R.* of window.)

PIM (*rising, calling*). Miss Marden! Miss Marden! (Looking at his
watch.) Yes, I think, Miss Marden, I had better go now and return a
little later. I have a telegram which I want to send, and perhaps by the
time I come back your uncle will be able--

DINAH (*coming to* PIM). Oh, but how disappointing of you, when we were
getting on together so nicely! And it was just going to be your turn to
tell me all about yourself.

PIM. I have really nothing to tell, Miss Marden. I have a letter of
introduction to your uncle, who in turn will give me, I hope, a letter to
a certain distinguished man whom it is necessary for me to meet. That is
all. (*Holding out his hand*.) And now, Miss Marden, I really think I'd
better be going.

DINAH (*taking his arm and hading him up stage* C. *to* L.). Oh, I'll
start you on your way to the post office.

PIM. Will you? Now, that's really very kind of you.

DINAH. No, it isn't.

PIM. Oh, but it is! You're a very kind little girl.

DINAH. I want to know if you're married--

PIM. Oh, no, I'm not married.

DINAH.--and all that sort of thing. You've got heaps to tell me, Mr. Pim. Have you got your hat? (PIM *shows his hat*.) Oh yes! That's right.

(BRIAN STRANGE *comes in from window up* R. *He is what* GEORGE calls a damned futuristic painter chap, aged 24. To look at he is a very pleasant boy, rather untidily dressed. He is about to tell *DINAH* the result of his interview with *GEORGE* when he catches sight of PIM.)

Then we'll--hullo, here's Brian! (*Crossing below and to his* R. seizing him.) Brian, this is Mr. Pim! Mr. Carraway Pim. He's been telling me all about himself.

PIM. I haven't said a word. I never opened my mouth.

DINAH. It's so interesting. He's just going to send a telegram, and then he's coming back again. Mr. Pim--(coyly and moving down to head of settee R.)--this is Brian--*you* know,

BRIAN (*nodding*). How-do-you-do?

PIM. How-do-you-do, sir?

DINAH (*pleadingly and crossing below* BRIAN *to* PIM), You won't mind going to the post office by yourself now, will you? (Coyly moving up to chair by writing-table and nervously kicking her ankle, etc.) Because, you see, Brian and I--(*She looks lovingly at* BRIAN.)

PIM (*moved to sentiment*). Miss Dinah and Mr.--er--Brian, I have only come into your lives for a moment, and it is probable that I shall now pass out of them for ever, but perhaps you will permit an old man--

DINAH. Oh, not so old!

PIM (*chuckling happily*). Not old? Well, shall we say a middle-aged man--(DINAH *nods assent*. PIM *laughs again*)--a middle-aged man to wish you both every happiness in the years that you have before you. (*Crossing in front of* DINAH, *shakes hands with* BRIAN.) Good-bye-- (*shaking hands with* DINAH)--good-bye, and thank you so much. Oh, I know
my way. (*Moving up* L. *and turning to* DINAH.) Turn to the left and down the hill? Turn to the left and down the hill.

(*Exit* PIM *up* L. DINAH *watches him off up* L. *on terrace and* BRIAN *up* R.)

DINAH (*coming into the room below writing-table to* R.C.). Brian, he'll get lost if he goes that way.

BRIAN (*crossing at back of windows and calling after him up* L.). Round to the left, sir. Yes, that's right. (He comes back into the room, crossing down L.C.) Rum old bird. Who is he?

DINAH. Darling, you haven't kissed me yet.

BRIAN (*moving up to her and pulling her down to below settee* L.), Oh, I say. I oughtn't to, but then one never ought to do the nice things.

DINAH. Why oughtn't you?

(*They sit on the sofa together--*BRIAN *to* R., DINAH *to* L.)

BRIAN. Well, we said we'd be good until we'd told your uncle and aunt all about it. You see, being a guest in their house--

DINAH. But, darling child, what *have* you been doing all this morning *except* telling George?

BRIAN. Oh, *trying* to tell George.

DINAH (*nodding*). Yes, of course, there's a difference.

BRIAN. I think he *guessed* there was something up, and he took me down to see the pigs--he said he had to see the pigs at once--I don't know why; an appointment perhaps. And we talked about pigs all the way, and I couldn't say, "Talking about pigs, I want to marry your niece--"

DINAH (*with mock indignation*). Oh, of course you couldn't.

BRIAN. No. Well, you see how it was. And then when we'd finished talking *about* pigs, we started talking *to* the pigs--

DINAH (*eagerly*). Oh, *how* is Arnold?

BRIAN. Arnold...? Oh yes, that's the little black-and-white one? He's very jolly, I believe, but naturally I wasn't thinking about him much. I was wondering how to begin. And then Lumsden came up, and wanted to talk
pig-food, and the atmosphere grew less and less romantic, and--and I gradually drifted away.

DINAH. Oh, poor darling! Well, we shall have to approach him through Olivia.

BRIAN. But I always wanted to tell her first; she's so much easier. Only *you* wouldn't let me.

DINAH. That's *your* fault, Brian. You would tell Olivia that she ought to have orange-and-black curtains in here.

BRIAN. But she wants orange and black curtains in here.

DINAH. Yes. (***Rising and standing with her back to fire, imitating***
GEORGE.) But George says he's not going to have any Futuristic nonsense
in an honest English country house, which has been good enough for his
father and his grandfather and his great-grandfather, and--and all the
rest of them. (***Kneels on settee***.) So there's a sort of strained feeling
between Olivia and George just now, and if Olivia were to--sort of
recommend you, well, it wouldn't do you much good.

BRIAN (***looking at her***). I see. Of course I know what ***you*** want, Dinah.

DINAH. What do I want?

BRIAN. You want a secret engagement--

DINAH. Oh!

BRIAN. And notes left under door-mats--

DINAH. Oh!

BRIAN. And meetings by the withered thorn--

DINAH. Oh!

BRIAN. When all the household is asleep.

DINAH. Oh!

BRIAN. I know you.

DINAH. Oh, but it is such fun! I love meeting people by withered thorns.

BRIAN. Well, I'm not going to have it.

DINAH (*childishly, sitting close to him*). Oh, George! Look at us being husbandy!

BRIAN. You babe! I adore you. (*He kisses her and holds her hands*.) You know, you're rather throwing yourself away on me. Do you mind?

DINAH (putting her legs up on settee and reclining her head on his shoulder). Not a bit.

BRIAN. We shall never be rich, but we shall have lots of fun, and meet interesting people, and feel that we're doing something worth doing, and not getting paid nearly enough for it, and we can curse the Academy together and the British Public, and--oh, it's an exciting life.

DINAH (*seeing it*). I shall love it.

BRIAN (*sincerely*). I'll make you love it. You shan't be sorry, Dinah.

DINAH. You shan't be sorry either, Brian.

BRIAN (*looking at her lovingly*). Oh, I know I shan't.... What will Olivia think about it? Will she be surprised?

DINAH. Olivia? Oh, she's never surprised. She always seems to have thought of things about half an hour before they happen. George just begins to get hold of them about half an hour after they've happened. (*Considering him, stroking his hair*.) After all, there's no reason why George shouldn't like you, darling.

BRIAN. I'm not his sort, you know, really.

DINAH. You're more Olivia's sort. Well, we'll tell Olivia this morning.

(OLIVIA *comes in from top of staircase up R*.)

OLIVIA (*coming in*). And what are you going to tell Olivia this morning? (*They jump up and go to her*.)

DINAH. Olivia, darling--

OLIVIA, Oh, well, I think I can guess,

(DINAH *goes to her* R, *and* BRIAN *to her* L., and they bring her down C.)

BRIAN (*following*). Say you understand, Mrs. Marden.

OLIVIA. Mrs. Marden, I am afraid, is a very dense person, Brian, but I think if you asked Olivia if she understood--

BRIAN. Bless you, Olivia. I *knew* you'd be on our side.

DINAH. Of course she would.

OLIVIA. I don't know if it's usual to kiss an aunt-in-law, Brian, but Dinah is such a very special sort of niece that--(she inclines her cheek and *BRIAN* kisses it).

DINAH (*backing away to* B. *a little*). I say, you are in luck to-day, Brian.

(BRIAN *moves up* C. *laughing*.)

OLIVIA (*crossing below settee* L. *and up* L. *to cabinet*). And how many people have been told the good news?

BRIAN. Nobody yet.

DINAH. Except Mr. Pim.

BRIAN (*crossing down to* DINAH). Oh, does he--

OLIVIA (*timing as she reaches cabinet, up* L.), Who's Mr, Pim?

DINAH. Oh, he just happened--(OLIVIA takes curtains and work-basket from
centre cupboard of cabinet.)--I say, are those the curtains? Then you're going to have them after all?

OLIVIA (with an air of surprise, coming down L., and putting work-basket on table L.C. and sitting with curtains). After all what? But I decided on them long ago. (*To* BRIAN.) You haven't told George yet.

BRIAN (*moving to below stool* L.C.). I began to, you know, but I never got any farther than "Er--there's just--er--"

DINAH (*crossing quickly below* OLIVIA *and speaking into her face*). George would talk about *pigs* all the time.

OLIVIA. Well, I suppose you want me to help you.

DINAH (*sitting to* L. *of* OLIVIA). Oh, do, darling.

BRIAN (*sits on stool* L.C.). It would be awfully decent of you. Of course, I'm not quite his sort really--

DINAH. You're my sort.

BRIAN. But I don't think he objects to me, and--

(GEORGE comes in from terrace, a typical, narrow-minded, honest country gentleman of forty odd. *BRIAN* rises hurriedly and crosses to above piano to *R. DINAH* rises and stands by fireplace. *OLIVIA* unfolds curtains and prepares to sew.)

GEORGE (*at the windows--he does not see* BRIAN). Hullo! Hullo! Hullo! What's all this about a Mr. Pim? Who is he? Where is he? (He puts his cap on table, and comes down, into room.) I had most important business with Lumsden, and the girl comes down and cackles about a Mr, Pim, or Ping, or something. Where did I put his card? (*Bringing it out*.) Carraway Pim. Never heard of him in my life, (Moves back to writing-table and puts down card.)

DINAH. He said he had a letter of introduction, Uncle George.

GEORGE. Oh, you saw him, did you! (*Comes down* C. *to* R.) Yes, that reminds me, there was a letter--(*he brings it out and reads it*).

DINAH. He had to send a telegram. He's coming back.

OLIVIA. Pass me those scissors, Brian.

BRIAN (*crossing to above table* L.C.). These? (*he passes them*.)

OLIVIA (*giving* BRIAN *a nod of encouragement and looking round at*

DINAH). Thank you.

GEORGE (*reading*). Ah well, a friend of Brymer's, Glad to oblige him. Yes, I know the man he wants. Coming back, you say, Dinah? (DINAH *nods*.) Then I'll be going back too. Send him down to the farm, Olivia, when he comes. (*Going up meets* BRIAN.) Hallo, what happened to you? (*Still moving up a little*.)

OLIVIA. Don't go, George, there's something we want to talk about. (DINAH *gives a long whistle. All look sheepish and* GEORGE notices their attitude.)

GEORGE. Hallo, what's this?

BRIAN (*quickly and over back of i.e. table to* OLIVIA). Shall I---! (DINAH *pantomimes. "Yes, do."*)

OLIVIA (*with a roguish loot at* DINAH). Yes, (*Sticks needle in work*.)

BRIAN (*stepping out to* C.) I've been wanting to tell you all this morning, sir, only I didn't seem to have an opportunity of getting it out.

GEORGE. Well, what is it?

(BRIAN, *taken aback for a moment, looks to* OLIVIA for encouragement. She nods approval and turning to *DINAH,* takes her hand encouragingly--)

BRIAN (*boldly*). I want to marry Dinah, sir.

GEORGE. You want to marry Dinah? God bless my soul!

DINAH (*rushing to him below and to his* R. and pulling her cheek against his coat, and her hands on his shoulder). Oh, do say you like the idea, Uncle George.

GEORGE. Like the idea! (*Taking her hands from his shoulder*.) Have you heard of this nonsense, Olivia?

(*Movement of annoyance from* DINAH.)

OLIVIA. They've just this moment told me, George. I think they would be happy together.

GEORGE (*crossing to fire-place* L., *to* BRIAN). And what do you propose to be happy together on?

BRIAN (R.C.). Well, of course, I know it doesn't amount to much at present, but we shan't starve.

DINAH. Brian got fifty pounds for a picture last March!

GEORGE (*a little upset by this*). Oh! (*Recovering gamely*.) And how many pictures have you sold since?

BRIAN (*gives a nervous look at* OLIVIA *and* DINAH, who then sits on settee R.). Well, none, but--

GEORGE. None! And I don't wonder. Who the devil is going to buy pictures with triangular clouds and square sheep? (BRIAN, *annoyed, moves up* R.C.) And they call that Art nowadays! Good God, man (moving up to the windows), go outside and look at the clouds!

OLIVIA (*busy stitching rings on curtains*). If he draws round clouds in future, George, will you let him marry Dinah?

(GEORGE *looks round, annoyed.* BRIAN *is hopeful and comes down towards*
DINAH.)

GEORGE (*upset by this, coming down to head of* L.C. *table*). What--
what? Yes, of course, you would be on his side--all this Futuristic
nonsense. (OLIVIA *commences to sew*.) I'm just taking these clouds as an
example. (*Crossing to* BRIAN.) I suppose I can see as well as any man in
the county, and I say that clouds aren't triangular.

BRIAN (*ingratiatingly*). After all, sir, at my age one is naturally
experimenting, and trying to find one's (with a laugh) --well, it sounds
priggish, but one's medium of expression. I shall find out what I want to
do directly, but I think I shall always be able to earn enough to live
on. Well, I have for the last three years.

GEORGE. I see, and now you want to experiment with a wife--

BRIAN. Yes--no--no--

DINAH. Yes, you do,

BRIAN. Yes.

GEORGE. And you propose to experimenting with my niece?

BRIAN (*with a shrug*). Well, of course, if you--

OLIVIA. You could help the experiment, darling, by giving Dinah a good
allowance until she's twenty-one.

GEORGE. Help the experiment! I don't *want* to help the experiment. (*Crossing up to writing-table*.)

OLIVIA (*apologetically*). Oh, I thought you did.

GEORGE. You will talk as if I was made of money. What with taxes always going up and rents always going down, it's as much as we can do to rub along as we are (*to back of* L.C. *table*), without making allowances to everybody who thinks she wants to get married. (*To* BRIAN.) And that's thanks to you, my friend.

BRIAN (*surprised*). To me?

OLIVIA. You never told me, darling. What's Brian been doing?

DINAH (*indignantly*). He hasn't been doing anything.

GEORGE (*round to foot of table* L.C.). He's one of your Socialists who go turning the country upside down.

OLIVIA. But even Socialists must get married sometimes.

GEORGE (*crossing below* OLIVIA *to fireplace*). I don't see any necessity.

OLIVIA. But you'd have nobody to damn after dinner, darling, if they all died out.

BRIAN (*coming a little* C.). Really, sir, I don't see what my politics and my art have got to do with it. I'm perfectly ready not to talk about either when I'm in your house, and as Dinah doesn't seem to object to them----

DINAH (*moving towards* BRIAN *and championing him*). I should think she
doesn't.

GEOEOE. Oh, you can get round the women, I daresay.

BRIAN. Well, it's Dinah I want to marry and live with. So what it really comes to is that you don't think I can support a wife.

GEORGE. Well, if you're going to do it by selling pictures, I don't think you can.

BRIAN (*moving to* R. *of table* L.C.). All right, tell me how much you want me to earn in a year, and I'll earn it.

GEORGE (*hedging*). It isn't merely a question of money. I just mention that as one thing--one of the important things. (GEORGE *crosses to* BRIAN *who backs towards* DINAH.) In addition to that, I think you are both too young to marry. (DINAH *stamps her foot*.) I don't think you know your own minds (DINAH *kneels dejectedly on settee* R.), and I am not at all persuaded that, with what I venture to call your outrageous tastes----

DINAH. Oh!

GEORGE You and my niece will live happily together. (Pause. Crossing up to writing-table, sits.) Just because she thinks she loves you, Dinah may persuade herself now that she agrees with all you say and do, but she has been properly brought up in an honest English country household-- (DINAH *throws up her arms and buries her face in her hands on piano*) and--er--she--well, in short, I cannot at all approve of any engagement between you. (*Getting up*.) Olivia, if this Mr.--er--Pim comes, I shall be down at the farm You might send him along to me.

(*He walks towards the windows up* L.)

BRIAN (*moving up* R., *followed by* DINAH; *indignantly*). Is there any reason why I shouldn't marry a girl who has been properly brought up?

GEORGE. I think you know my views, Strange.

(DINAH, *disappointed, crosses down* R. *again to below table* R.C.)

OLIVIA. George, wait a moment, dear. We can't quite leave it like this.

GEORGE. I have said all I want to say on the subject.

(DINAH *sits on settee* R.)

OLIVIA. Yes, darling, but I haven't begun to say all that *I* want to say on the subject.

GEORGE (*crossing down to back of table* L.C.). Of course, if you have anything to say, Olivia, I will listen to it; but I don't know that this is quite the time--(OLIVIA makes a marked movement as she is sewing the curtains), or that you have chosen--(*looking darkly at the curtains*)-- quite the occupation likely to--er--endear your views to me.

DINAH (mutinously, rising quickly and crossing to stool on which she kneels and looks up into **GEORGE'S** face and bangs the table). I may as well tell you, Uncle George, that I have got a good deal to say, too.

(BRIAN *crosses down to her* R., gingerly pulling her sleeve, trying to restrain her.)

OLIVIA. Yes, darling. I can guess what you are going to say, Dinah, and I think you had better keep it for the moment.

DINAH (*meekly, backing to* R. *below* BRIAN *and to* L. *of table* R.C.). Yes, Aunt Olivia.

OLIVIA. Brian, you might take her outside for a walk. I expect you have plenty to talk about.

(BRIAN *and* DINAH *move up* R.)

GEORGE (*following them up*). Now mind, Strange, no love-making. I put you on your honour about that.

BRIAN (*looking round dubiously at* DINAH). I'll do my best to avoid it, sir.

DINAH (*cheekily*). May I take his arm if we go up a hill?

OLIVIA. I'm sure you'll know how to behave--both of you.

BRIAN (R. *of writing-table*). Come on, then, Dinah.

DINAH (*following him*). Right-o. (They exeunt through windows and off to L.)

GEORGE (*as they go*). And if you do see any clouds, Strange, take a good look at them. (*He chuckles to himself*.) Triangular clouds--I never heard of such nonsense. (He goes back to his chair at the writing-table and sits.) Futuristic rubbish... Well, Olivia?

OLIVIA (*sewing curtains*). Well, George?

GEORGE. What are you doing?

OLIVIA. Making curtains--(*grunt of disapproval from* GEORGE)--George. Won't they be rather sweet? Oh, but I forgot--you don't like them.

GEORGE. No. I don't like them, and what is more, I don't mean to have them in my house. As I told you yesterday, this is the house of a simple country gentleman, and I don't want any of these new-fangled ideas in it.

OLIVIA. Is marrying for love a new-fangled idea?

GEORGE. We'll come to that directly. None of you women can keep to the point. What I am saying now is that the house of my fathers and forefathers is good enough for me.

OLIVIA. Do you know, George, I can hear one of your ancestors saying that to his wife in their smelly old cave--(GEORGE looks up annoyed at her levity)--when the new-fangled idea of building houses was first suggested. "The Cave of my Forefathers is good enough for----"

GEORGE (*rising and coming to* R. *of* L.C. *table*). That's ridiculous. Naturally we must have progress. But that's just the point. (Indicating the curtains.) I don't call this sort of thing progress. It's--ah--retrogression.

OLIVIA. Well, anyhow, it's pretty.

GEORGE. There I disagree with you. And I must say once more that I will not have them hanging in my house. (*Going up* R.C.)

OLIVIA. Very well, George. (*But she goes on working*.)

GEORGE (*seeing her continuing to sew, stops*). That being so, I don't see the necessity of going on with them.

OLIVIA. Well, I must do something with them now I've got the material.

(GEORGE *goes up to writing-table, sits and writes*.)

I thought perhaps I could sell them when they're finished--as we're so poor.

GEORGE (*turns to her with surprised look*). What do you mean--so poor?

OLIVIA. Well, you said just now that you couldn't give Dinah an allowance because rents had gone down.

GEORGE (*annoyed*). Confound it, Olivia! Keep to the point! We'll talk about Dinah's affairs directly. We're discussing our own affairs at the moment.

OLIVIA. But what is there to discuss, dear?

GEORGE. Well, those ridiculous things.

OLIVIA. But we've finished that. You've said you wouldn't have them hanging in your house, and I've said, "Very well, George."--(GEORGE is again annoyed.)--Now we can go on to Dinah, and Brian.

GEORGE (*shouting*). But put these beastly things away.

OLIVIA (*rising and gathering up the curtains*). Very well, George.

(*Going up* L. *she places the curtains on the cabinet*.)

GEORGE (waits impatiently until she has put them away on top of cabinet). Ah! That's better.

(OLIVIA *comes to table* L.C., closes her workbox and then crosses down to settee R.)

GEORGE (*rising and crossing down to* OLIVIA and placing arms lovingly on her shoulder). Now look here, Olivia, old girl, you've been a jolly good wife to me--(*takes his arms from her shoulder*)--and we don't often have rows, and if I've been rude to you about this--lost my temper a bit perhaps, what?--I'll say I'm sorry. May I have a kiss?

OLIVIA (*holding up her face*). George, darling! (*He kisses her.*) Do you love me?

GEORGE. You know I do, old girl.

OLIVIA. As much as Brian loves Dinah?

GEORGE (*stiffly, taking her hands from his shoulders*). I've said all I want to say about that. (*He goes away from her to* L.)

OLIVIA. Oh, but there must be lots you want to say and perhaps don't like to. (*Sits on settee* R.) Do tell me, darling.

GEORGE (*coming back to* C.). What it comes to is this. I consider that Dinah is too young to choose a husband for herself, and that Strange isn't the husband I should choose for her.

OLIVIA. You were calling him Brian yesterday.

GEORGE. Yesterday I regarded him as a boy, now he wants me to look upon him as a man.

OLIVIA. He's twenty-four.

GEORGE. Yes, and Dinah's nineteen. Ridiculous. (Crossing up to smoking-table up *R.,* and filling his pipe which he finds on table.)

OLIVIA. If he'd been a Conservative, and thought that clouds were round, I suppose he'd have seemed older, somehow.

GEORGE. That's a different point altogether. That has nothing to do with his age.

OLIVIA (*innocently*). Oh, I thought it had.

GEORGE (*crossing down* C. *stuffing tobacco into his pipe*). What I am objecting to is these ridiculously early marriages before either party knows its own mind, much less the mind of the other party. (Moving to fireplace looking for a match.) Such marriages invariably lead to unhappiness.

OLIVIA. Of course, *my* first marriage wasn't a happy one.

GEORGE. As you know, Olivia, I dislike speaking about your first marriage at all--(*takes a match from table down* L. OLIVIA rises slowly and goes up to *R.* of writing-table)--and I had no intention of bringing it up now, but since you mention it--well, there's a case in point. (Sits on settee *L.,* lighting his pipe.)

OLIVIA (*looking back at it*). When I was eighteen, I was in love.

GEORGE (*turning to her*). What?

OLIVIA. Or perhaps I only thought I was, and I don't know if I should

have been happy or not if I had married him. But my father made me marry Mr. Jacob Telworthy. (GEORGE ***looks up at her, annoyed***.) And when things
were too hot for him in England--"too hot for him"--I think that was the expression we used in those days--then we went to Australia, and I left him there. (***Goes slowly down to back of settee*** L.) And the only happy moment I had in all my married life was on the morning when I saw in the papers that he was dead. (***Leans with her arms over back of settee***.)

GEORGE (very uncomfortable yet lovingly taking her hands with his left hand). Yes, yes, my dear, I know, I know. You must have had a terrible time. I can hardly bear to think about it. My only hope is that I have made up to you for it in some degree. (She places her left cheek lovingly on his head.) (***Dropping her hands***.) But I don't see what bearing it has upon Dinah's case.

OLIVIA. Oh, none, except that *my* father *liked* Jacob's political opinions and his views on art. (***Moving slowly round*** L.C. table to below stool at foot.) I expect that that was why he chose him for me.

GEORGE. You seem to think that I wish to choose a husband for Dinah. I don't at all. Let her choose whom she likes as long as he can support her and there's a chance of their being happy together. Now, with regard to this fellow--

OLIVIA. You mean Brian?

GEORGE. Well, he's got no money, and he's been brought up in quite a different way from Dinah. Dinah may be prepared to believe that--er--all cows are blue, and that--er--waves are square, but she won't go on believing it for ever.

OLIVIA. Neither will Brian.

GEORGE (*moving to* R. *end of settee*). Well, that's what I keep telling him, only he won't see it. Just as I keep telling you about those ridiculous curtains. (Points to cupboard with pipe in right hand over his left shoulder.) It seems to me that I am the only person in the house with any eyesight left.

OLIVIA. Perhaps you are, darling; but you must let us find out our own mistakes for ourselves. (*Sits on stool* L.C.) At any rate, Brian is a gentleman; he loves Dinah, Dinah loves him; he's earning enough to support himself, and you are earning enough to support Dinah.

GEORGE (*amazed*). What?

OLIVIA. I think it's worth risking, George.

GEORGE (*stiffly*). I can only say the whole question demands much more anxious thought than you seem to have given it. You say that he is a gentleman. He knows how to behave, I admit; but if his morals are as topsy-turvy as his tastes and--er--politics, as I've no doubt they are (*rising and moving to* L.), then-er--In short, I do *not* approve of Brian Strange as a husband for my niece and ward. (*Knocks pipe out down* L.)

OLIVIA (*looking at him thoughtfully*). You *are* a curious mixture, George. You were so very unconventional when you married me, and you're so very conventional when Brian wants to marry Dinah.... George Marden to marry the widow of a convict!

GEORGE (*advancing*). Convict! What do you mean?

OLIVIA. Jacob Telworthy, convict--I forget his number--surely I told you all this, dear, when we got engaged?

GEORGE. Never!

OLIVIA. Oh, but I told you how he carelessly put the wrong signature to a cheque for a thousand pounds in England; how he made a little mistake about two or three companies he'd promoted in Australia; and how--

GEORGE. Yes, yes (*crossing slowly to* C. *below* OLIVIA), but you never told me he'd been--er--well-- *convicted*!

OLIVIA. What difference does it make?

GEORGE. My dear Olivia, if you can't see that--a--a--oh, well!

OLIVIA. Oh! A convict! So, you see, we needn't be too particular about our niece, need we?

GEORGE. I think we had better leave your first husband out of the conversation altogether. I never wished to refer to him; I never wish to hear about him again. I certainly had not realized that he was actually--er--well--convicted for his--er--(moving to writing-table and picking up his cap).

OLIVIA. Mistakes. GEORGE. Well, we needn't go into that. As for this other matter, I don't for a moment take it seriously. Dinah is an exceptionally pretty girl, and young. Strange is a good-looking boy. (*Coming down to back of settee* L.) If they are attracted to each other, it is a mere outward attraction which I am convinced will not lead to any lasting happiness. (OLIVIA *is about to protest*.) That must be regarded as my last word in the matter, Olivia. If this Mr.--er--what was his name, comes, I shall be down at the farm. (GEORGE goes out by the staircase up R.)

(*Left alone,* OLIVIA *rises, goes up* C., takes up her curtains again and crossing down *L.* sits on settee, and gets calmly to work upon them.)

(DINAH *comes in by the windows from up* R. *and crosses to* L. window at back, then seeing *OLIVIA,* beckons to *BRIAN* and runs down to back of settee to *R.* of *OLIVIA. BRIAN* enters from up *R.,* and follows down to back of table L.C.)

DINAH (*over back of settee*). Finished?

OLIVIA (*startled*). Oh, no, I've got all these rings to put on.

DINAH. I meant talking to George.

OLIVIA. Oh!

BRIAN. We walked about outside----

DINAH. Until we heard him *not* talking to you any more----

BRIAN. And we didn't kiss each other once.

DINAH AND BRIAN (*pointing roguishly and with satisfaction at* OLIVIA). Ah!

DINAH. Brian was very George-like. He wouldn't even let me tickle the back of his neck. (*She goes suddenly to* OLIVIA *and sits on her* L.) Darling (*putting her arms round* OLIVIA *and kissing her*), being George-like is a very nice thing to be--I mean a nice thing for other people to be--I mean--oh, you know what I mean. But say that he's going to be decent about it.

OLIVIA. Of course he is, Dinah.

BRIAN (*sits on stool* L.C., *and leans forward eagerly*). You mean he'll let me come here as--as----

DINAH. As my young man?

OLIVIA. Oh, I think so.

DINAH (*kissing* OLIVIA). Olivia, you're a wonder.

(*Embraces her round the neck*.)

(*Rising and crossing below* BRIAN, *touching him on the shoulder*.)

Brian!

(Crossing to piano, sits and plays five bars of "The Wedding March," rises and crosses at back of *BRIAN* to *L.* of *OLIVIA* behind settee.)

Have you really talked him round?

OLIVIA. I haven't said anything yet.

DINAH (*very disappointed*). Oh!

(BRIAN *rises and backs to* C.)

OLIVIA. But I dare say I shall think of something.

BRIAN. Oh! my lord.

DINAH (*disappointedly*). Oh!

BRIAN (*going up* C.). After all, Dinah, I'm going back to London to-morrow----

DINAH (*crossing quickly towards* BRIAN). Oh, no, no!

OLIVIA. Now, Dinah. You can be good for one more day, and then when Brian
isn't here, we'll see what we can do.

DINAH (*placing her hands on* BRIAN'S *shoulders*). Yes, but I didn't want him to go back to-morrow.

BRIAN (*sternly, taking her hands away*). Must. Hard work before me. (DINAH *moves to back of table* L.C.) Earn thousands a year. (Going down *R. DINAH* and *OLIVIA* are amused). Paint the Mayor and Corporation of Pudsey, life-size, including chains of office; paint slice of haddock on plate. Copy Landseer for old gentleman in Bayswater. Design antimacassar for middle-aged sofa in Streatham. (Sitting and putting his legs up on settee R.) Oh, yes. Earn a living for you. Dinah.

DINAH (*giggling*). Oh, Brian, you're heavenly. What fun we shall have when we're married.

BRIAN (*with exaggerated dignity*). Sir Brian Strange, R.A., if you please, Miss Marden. Sir Brian Strange, R.A., writes: "Your Sanogene has proved a most excellent tonic. After completing the third acre of my Academy picture, 'The Mayor and Corporation of Pudsey,' I was completely exhausted, but one bottle of Sanogene revived me, and I finished the remaining seven acres at a single sitting."

OLIVIA (*rising and looking about her*). Brian, find my scissors for me.
(*Sits again*.)

BRIAN (*rising and crossing to* C.). Scissors. Sir Brian Strange, R.A.,
looks for scissors.

(BRIAN, clasping his hands behind his back, with a very important walk,
looks first on the top end of piano, then on writing-table at back.
DINAH *playfully follows him round, imitating his walk*. BRIAN crosses
to cabinet up L. and finds the scissors on top, takes them up and in a
threatening attitude turns to *DINAH,* exclaiming, *"Ha, ha!" DINAH* with
a little playful scream backs to chair below writing-table, and sits.
Holding up scissors.)

Once more we must record an unqualified success for the eminent
Academician. (*Turning to* OLIVIA and with a bow hands them over the
back of settee to her.) Your scissors.

OLIVIA. Thank you so much.

DINAH. Come on, Brian, let's go out. I feel open-airy.

(*They go up* R.)

OLIVIA. Don't be late for lunch, there's good people. Lady Marden is
coming.

DINAH. Aunt Juli-ah! Help! (*She faints in* BRIAN'S *arms*.) That means
a clean pinafore. Brian, you'll jolly well have to brush your hair.

BRIAN (*feeling it*). I suppose there's no time now to go up to London and get it cut?

(*Enter* ANNE from stairs up R. and comes to foot of staircase, followed by *PIM,* who comes half-way down the stairs.)

ANNE. Mr. Pim!

DINAH (*delighted*). Hullo. Mr. Pim! (*Imitating a clown*.) Here we are again! You can't get rid of us so easily, you see.

PIM. I--er--dear Miss Marden----(*Crosses down to* C.)

OLIVIA. How-do-you-do, Mr. Pim? I can't get up, but do come and sit down (PIM *shakes hands with* OLIVIA.) My husband will be here in a minute. Anne, send somebody down to the farm----

ANNE, I think I heard the Master in the library, madam.

OLIVIA. Oh, will you tell him then?

ANNE. Yes, madam,

(ANNE *goes out up staircase*.)

OLIVIA. You'll stay to lunch, of course, Mr. Pim?

DINAH (*coming down* C. *to* R.) Oh, do!

PIM. It's very kind of you, Mrs. Marden, but-----

DINAH. Oh, you simply must, Mr. Pim. You haven't told us half enough about yourself yet. I want to hear all about your early life.

OLIVIA. Dinah!

(DINAH sits at piano and plays thirty-two bars of "If you could only care.")

PIM. Oh, we are almost, I might say, old friends, Mrs. Marden.

(BRIAN **comes down and kneels on settee** R., **listening to** DINAH **playing**.)

DINAH. Of course we are. He knows Brian, too. There's more in Mr. Pim than you think. You will stay to lunch, won't you?

PIM. (**sits on stool** L.C.) It's very kind of you to ask me, Mrs. Marden, but I am lunching with the Trevors.

OLIVIA. Oh, well, you must come to lunch another day.

PIM. Oh, thank you, thank you.

DINAH. The reason why we like Mr. Pim so much is that he was the first person to congratulate us. We feel that he is going to have a great influence on our lives.

PIM. (**to** OLIVIA). I, so to speak, stumbled on the engagement this morning, and--er--

OLIVIA. I see. Children, you must go and tidy yourselves up. Run along.

BRIAN. Sir Brian and Lady Strange never run; they walk.

(DINAH **stops playing**.) (**Offering his** R. **arm and bowing**.) Madam!

(DINAH *curtsies and takes his arm and they go up* C.)

(DINAH *takes mincing steps and playfully shakes her hand at* MR. PIM, *who is amused*.)

DINAH. Au revoir, Mr. Pim. (*Dramatically*.) We--shall--meet-- *again*!

(PIM. *laughing heartily, rises and bows*.)

(BRIAN *and* DINAH *go out through the window up* C. *to* L.)

OLIVIA. You must forgive them, Mr. Pim. They're such children. And naturally they're rather excited just now.

PIM. Oh, naturally, naturally!

OLIVIA. Of course you won't say anything about their engagement. We only heard about it five minutes ago, and nothing has been settled yet.

PIM. Of course, of course!

(*Enter* GEORGE *from staircase up* R.)

GEORGE. Ah, Mr. Pim, we meet at last. Sorry to have kept you waiting before. (*Shaking hands*.) How are you? How are you?

PIM. The apology should come from me, Mr. Marden, for having--er--

GEORGE. Not at all. Very glad to meet you now. Any friend of Brymer's. You want a letter to this man Fanshawe?

OLIVIA. Shall I be in your way at all?

PIM. Oh, no, no, please don't.

GEOBGE. Oh, no. It's only just a question of a letter. Fanshawe will put you in the way of seeing all that you want to see. (Crossing up to writing-table, sits.) He's a very old friend of mine. (Taking a sheet of notepaper and turning in chair to PIM.) You'll stay to lunch, of course?

PIM. It's very kind of you, but I'm lunching with the Trevors. (Sits settee R. and puts down his hat and gloves.)

GEORGE. Ah, well, they'll look after you all right. Good chap, Trevor.

PIM. Oh, very good ... very good. (*To* OLIVIA.) You see, Mrs. Marden, I have only recently arrived from Australia--(OLIVIA stops in her sewing and *GEORGE* looks up)--after travelling about the world for some years, and I'm rather out of touch with my--er--fellow-workers in London.

OLIVIA. I see! You've been in Australia, Mr. Pim?

PIM. Oh, yes, I----

GEORGE (*after a loud cough*). Sorry to keep you waiting, Mr. Pim. I shan't be a moment.

PIM. Oh, that's all right, thank you. (*To* OLIVIA.) Oh, yes, I have been in Australia more than once in the last few years.

OLIVIA. Really? I used to live at Sydney many years ago. Do you know Sydney at all?

PIM. Oh, yes, I was----

GEORGE (*coughing*). H'r'm! Perhaps I'd better mention that you are a friend of the Trevors?

PIM. Thank you, thank you. (*To* OLIVIA.) Indeed yes, I spent several months in Sydney a few years ago.

OLIVIA. How curious! I wonder if we have any friends in common there.

GEORGE (*coughing and gruffly*). Extremely unlikely, I should think. Sydney is a very big place.

PIM. True, true, but the world is a very small place, Mr. Marden. I had a remarkable instance of that, coming over on the boat this last time.

GEORGE. Ah! (Feeling that the conversation is now safe, he resumes his letter.)

PIM. Yes. There was a man I used to employ in Sydney some years ago, a bad fellow, I'm afraid, Mrs. Marden, who had been in prison for some kind of fraudulent company-promoting and had taken to drink and--and so on.

OLIVIA. Yes, yes, I understand.

PIM. Drinking himself to death, I should have said. I gave him at the most another year to live. Yet to my amazement the first person I saw as I stepped on board the boat that brought me to England last week was this fellow. There was no mistaking him. I spoke to him, in fact; we recognized each other.

(GEORGE *rises*.)

OLIVIA. Really?

PIM. He was travelling steerage; we didn't meet again on board, and as it happened at Marseilles, this poor fellow--er--now what was his name? A very unusual one. Began with a--a T, I think.

OLIVIA (*with suppressed feeling*). Yes, Mr. Pim, yes? (She puts out a hand to GEORGE.)

GEORGE (*in an undertone, taking her hand*). Nonsense, dear!

PIM (*triumphantly*). I've got it! Telworthy!

OLIVIA (*draws back in settee, overcome*). Telworthy!

GEORGE. Good God!

PIM (*a little surprised at the success of his story*). An unusual name, is it not? Not a name you could forget when once you had heard it.

OLIVIA (*with feeling, gazing into space with hands clenched*). No, it is not a name you could forget when once you had heard it.

GEORGE (*hastily coming over to* PIM). Quite so, Mr. Pim, a most remarkable name, a most odd story altogether. Well, well, here's your letter--(PIM *rises and tales letter*)--and if you're sure you won't stay to lunch----

PIM. No, thank you. You see, I'm lunching with----

GEORGE. With the Trevors, yes. I remember you told me. (Taking his arm and hurrying him up C.) I'll just see you on your way.... (*To* OLIVIA, *who does not notice* PIM *holding out his hand to say good-bye*.) Er--my dear----

OLIVIA (*holding out her hand, but not looking at him*). Good-bye, Mr. Pim.

PIM (*shaking hands with* OLIVIA). Good-bye, good-bye!

GEORGE (*taking him by the arm up* L. *towards the windows*). This way, this way. Quicker for you.

PIM, Thank you, thank you.

(GEORGE *hurries him up* C. *and he exits to* L. OLIVIA looks into the past and shudders. *GEORGE* comes back to C.)

GEORGE. Good God! Telworthy! (ANNE *enters from up* R. and comes to foot
of staircase.) Is it possible?

(*Before* OLIVIA *can answer,* LADY MARDEN *is announced*.)

ANNE. Lady Marden.

(GEORGE *crosses down to* OLIVIA and touches her on the shoulder. They pull themselves together, and *OLIVIA* rises and is crossing towards C. *to greet* LADY MARDEN, *who does not appear*.)

QUICK CURTAIN.

ACT II

SCENE.-- The same scene and furniture with addition of a camp table and five camp chairs outside on terrace at back centre. Lunch is over. LADY MARDEN'S *whip and gloves are on writing-table*.

(ANNE *enters with coffee for five on salver, from double doors* R., and is about to place it on table *L.C.* when *OLIVIA,* who follows her on, says:)

OLIVIA. We'll have coffee on the terrace, Anne.

ANNE. Very good, madam. (*Moves up* L. and places salver on camp table on terrace.)

(LADY MARDEN *follows* OLIVIA *from double doors* R. ANNE crosses at back of windows to R.)

OLIVIA. We'll have coffee on the terrace, Aunt Julia.

(LADY MARDEN *crosses in front of* OLIVIA *and up* L. through windows and sits *R.* at back of camp table. *GEORGE* follows LADY MARDEN, *meets* OLIVIA, *and both throw up their arms despairingly.* OLIVIA *crosses up* L. *through windows and sits to* L. *of camp table.* DINAH *and* BRIAN *follow* GEORGE *on*.)

(ANNE *exits at doors* R.)

(GEORGE *turns, and seeing* DINAH *is annoyed, follows* OLIVIA *up* L. *and sits* L. *of* LADY MARDEN.)

DINAH (*to* BRIAN). I know Aunt Julia likes a little music.

(DINAH *comes down to piano and takes up small guitar.* BRIAN crosses to *L.,* laughing at her. She goes up *L.* of writing-table, playing and singing, and crosses round back of writing-table and sits to *R.* of camp table, *BRIAN* follows her and stands with his back to windows. GEORGE *and* LADY MARDEN *are annoyed with* DINAH'S playing, and tell her to stop, and she does so. *OLIVIA* pours milk into *DINAH'S* cup and BRIAN passes it to her; she drinks and then commences to play again and is stopped by looks from *LADY MARDEN* and GEORGE.)

LADY MARDEN (*to* DINAH). No! No! Don't do it!

OLIVIA. Your aunt does not like it, dear.

(GEORGE *and* OLIVIA *want to be alone, so do* BRIAN *and* DINAH. At last *BRIAN* murmurs something about a cigarette-case, and catching DINAH'S *eye, comes into the room. He leans against the sofa down* L. *and waits for her*.)

DINAH (*loudly, as she comes in strumming on guitar*). Have you found it?

BRIAN. Found what?

DINAH (*in her ordinary voice, crossing quickly down to* BRIAN). That was just for *their* benefit. I said I'd help you find it. It *is* your cigarette-case we're looking for, isn't it?

BRIAN (*taking it out*). Yes. Have one?

DINAH. No, thank you, darling. (BRIAN *goes up* R. in smoking-table for a match.) Aunt Juli-ah still thinks it's unladylike.... Have you ever seen her beagling? (*Comes down to piano, puts down instrument*.)

BRIAN. No. Is that very ladylike?

DINAH (*sitting on settee* R.). Very.... I say, what has happened, do you think?

BRIAN (*moving down to back of table* R.C.). Everything. I love you, and you love me.

DINAH. Silly! I meant between George and Olivia. Didn't you notice them at lunch?

BRIAN (*sits on table*). I noticed that you seemed to be doing most of the talking. But then I've noticed that before sometimes. Do you think Olivia and your uncle have quarrelled because of *us*?

DINAH. Of course not. George may *think* he has quarrelled, but I'm quite sure Olivia hasn't. No (DINAH *beckons to* BRIAN, who comes and sits above her), I believe Mr. Pim's at the bottom of it. He's brought some terribly sad news about George's investments. (*Rising and facing* BRIAN.) The old home will have to be sold up.

BRIAN. Good. Then your uncle won't mind your marrying me.

DINAH (*by table above settee* R.). Yes, darling, but you must be more dramatic about it than that. "George," you must say, with tears in your eyes, "I cannot pay off the whole of the mortgage for you. I have only two and ninepence; but at least let me take your niece off your hands." Then George will (hitting him on the shoulder) thump you on the back and say gruffly (***crossing to*** L.), "You're a good fellow, Brian, a damn good fellow," and he'll blow his nose very loudly, and say, "Confound this cigar, it won't draw properly."

BRIAN (***rising and crossing to*** DINAH). Dinah, you're a heavenly idiot. And you've simply got to marry me, uncles or no uncles.

DINAH. Hush! (***She takes his hand and they sit on settee*** L., hiding from others at back). It will have to be "uncles," I'm afraid, because, you see, I'm his ward, and I can get sent to Chancery or Coventry or somewhere beastly, if I marry without his consent, Haven't ***you*** got anybody who objects to your marrying ***me***?

BRIAN. Nobody, thank Heaven.

DINAH. Well, that's rather disappointing of you. I saw myself fascinating your aged father at the same time that you were fascinating George. I should have done it much better than you. As a George-fascinator you aren't very successful, sweetheart.

BRIAN (***kissing her hand***). What am I like as a Dinah-fascinator?

DINAH. Plus six, darling.

BRIAN. Then I'll stick to that and leave George to Olivia.

DINAH. I expect she'll manage him all right. I have great faith in Olivia. But you'll marry me, anyhow, won't you, Brian?

BRIAN. I will.

DINAH. Even if we have to wait till I'm twenty-one?

BRIAN. Even if we have to wait till you're fifty-one.

DINAH (*holding out her hands to him*). Darling!

BRIAN (*uneasily*). I say, don't do that.

DINAH. Why not?

BRIAN. Well, I promised I wouldn't kiss you.

DINAH. Oh! (*Rising and crossing to* C., *watching the others at back*). Well, you might just send me a kiss. You can look the other way as if you didn't know I was here.

BRIAN. Like this?

(He looks the other way, kisses the tips of his fingers, and flicks it carelessly in her direction. She pretends to catch it, kissing her own hands.)

DINAH. That was a lovely one. Now here's one coming for you.

(She throws him a kiss. He catches it gracefully and conveys it to his mouth.)

BRIAN (*rising, and with a low bow*). Madam, I thank you.

DINAH (*curtsying*). Your servant, Mr. Strange,

OLIVIA (*rising from outside*). Dinah!

DINAH (*jumping up*). Hullo! (*Moving quickly to piano, plays "Mickey."*)

(BRIAN *throws away his cigarette and walks to* L.)

(OLIVIA *comes in through the window up* L., *followed by* GEORGE *and* LADY MARDEN, the latter a vigorous young woman of sixty odd, who always
looks as if she were beagling.)

OLIVIA (*coming down to* DINAH *above piano*). Aunt Julia wants to see the pigs, dear. I wish you'd take her down. I'm rather tired, and your uncle has some business to attend to.

(GEORGE *sits in chair up* C. *in front of writing-table*.)

LADY MARDEN (*moving down* C.), I've always said that you don't take enough exercise, Olivia. (*Turning to others*.) Look at me--sixty-five and proud of it. (*Goes up* R. and takes up gloves and riding-whip from writing-table.)

OLIVIA (*taking off her coatee*). Yes, Aunt Julia, you're wonderful.

DINAH. How old would Olivia be if she took exercise?

(OLIVIA, *smiling, but with an admonishing look at* DINAH, *comes up* R. *and places her coatee on balustrade*.)

GEORGE (*from up* C.). Don't fool about asking silly questions, Dinah. Your aunt hasn't much time.

BRIAN. May I come, too, Lady Marden?

LADY MARDEN (*coming down centre to* BRIAN). Well, a little exercise wouldn't do *you* any harm, Mr. Strange. You're an artist, ain't you?

(DINAH *stops playing*.)

BRIAN. Well, I try to paint.

DINAH (*rises and moves to* R.C.). He sold a picture last March for----

GEORGE. Yes, yes, never mind that now.

LADY MARDEN. Yes, unhealthy life. (*Going to* R. of writing-table and crossing at back, turns to *DINAH* and BRIAN.) Well, come along.

(*She strides out up* L., *followed by* DINAH *and* BRIAN, *who upset* GEORGE'S *papers on writing-table as they go*. OLIVIA takes the curtains and workbox from *C.* cupboard of cabinet and comes down L.)

GEORGE (*looking up and seeing* OLIVIA). Really, Olivia, we've got something more important, more vital to us than curtains, to discuss, now that we *are* alone at last.

OLIVIA. I wasn't going to discuss them, dear. (*Sits*.)

GEORGE. Of course, I'm always glad to see Aunt Julia in my house, but I wish she hadn't chosen this day of all days to come to lunch.

OLIVIA. It wasn't Aunt Julia's fault. It was really Mr. Pim who chose the wrong day.

GEORGE (*fiercely and rising*). Good heavens, is it true?

OLIVIA. About Jacob Telworthy?

GEORGE. Yon told me he was dead. (***Moving down to*** L. *of* L.C. ***table***.) You always said that he was dead.

OLIVIA. Well, I always thought that he was dead. He was as dead as anybody could be. All the papers said he was dead.

GEORGE (***scornfully***). The papers!(Crossing up to smoking-table for his pipe.)

OLIVIA (***as if this would settle it for*** GEORGE). The ***Times*** said he was dead. There was a paragraph about him. Apparently even his death was fraudulent.

GEORGE (***coming down*** C.). Yes, yes, I'm not blaming you, Olivia, but what are we going to do, that's the question, what are we going to do? My God, it's horrible! (***Crossing to fireplace***.) You've never been married to me at all! You don't seem to understand.

OLIVIA. It is a little difficult to realize. You see, it doesn't seem to have made any difference to our happiness.

GEORGE. No, that's what's so terrible. (OLIVIA ***looks up surprised***.) I mean--well, of course, we were quite innocent in the matter. (Sits in arm-chair down L.) But, at the same time, nothing can get over the fact that we--we had no right to--to be happy.

OLIVIA. Would you rather we had been miserable?

GEORGE. You're Telworthy's wife, that's what you don't seem to understand. You're Telworthy's wife. You--er--forgive me, Olivia, but it's the horrible truth--you committed bigamy when you married me. (In horror, going up L.) Bigamy! (***Coming round to*** C.)

OLIVIA. It is an ugly word, isn't it?

GEORGE. Yes, but you don't understand. (***Coming quickly down*** C., sits on stool *L.C.,* facing her.) Look here, Olivia, old girl, the whole thing is nonsense, eh? It isn't your husband, it's some other Telworthy that this fellow met. That's right, isn't it? Some other shady swindler who turned up on the boat, eh? This sort of thing doesn't happen to people like *us*--committing bigamy and all that. Some other fellow.

OLIVIA (***shaking her head***). I knew all the shady swindlers in Sydney.... They came to dinner.... There were no others called Telworthy.

GEORGE (***rising with gesture of despair***). Well, what are we going to do?

OLIVIA. You sent Mr. Pim away so quickly. He might have told us things. Telworthy's plans. Where he is now. You hurried him away so quickly.

GEORGE. I've sent a note round to ask him to come back. My one idea at the moment was to get him out of the house--to hush things up. (Going up to writing-table.)

OLIVIA. You can't hush up two husbands.

GEORGE (***in despair***). You can't. (***Sits at writing-table***.) Everybody will know. Everybody!

OLIVIA. The children, Aunt Julia, they may as well know now as later. Mr. Pim must, of course.

GEORGE. I do not propose to discuss my private affairs with Mr. Pim----

OLIVIA. But he's mixed himself up in them rather, hasn't he, and if you're going to ask him questions----

GEORGE. I only propose to ask him one question. I shall ask him if he is absolutely certain of this fellow's name. I can do that quite easily without letting him know the reason for my inquiry.

OLIVIA. You couldn't make a mistake about a name like Telworthy. But he might tell us something about Telworthy's plans. Perhaps he's going back to Australia at once. Perhaps he thinks I'm dead, too. Perhaps--oh, there are so many things I want to know.

GEORGE. Yes, yes, dear. It would be interesting to--that is, one naturally wants to know these things, but of course it doesn't make any real difference.

OLIVIA (*surprised*). No difference?

GEORGE (*rising and coming down to back of settee* L.). Well, that is to say, you're as much his wife if he's in Australia as you are if he's in England.

OLIVIA. I am not his wife at all. (*Shaking her head*.) Jacob Telworthy may be alive, but I am not his wife. I ceased to be his wife when I became yours.

GEORGE. You never *were* my wife. (*Annoyed and crossing to* R. and back again to L.C.) That is the terrible part of it. Our union--you make me say it, Olivia--has been unhallowed by the Church. Unhallowed even by the Law. Legally, we have been living in--living in--well, the point is, how does the Law stand? I imagine that Telworthy could get a--a divorce....

Oh, it seems impossible that things like this can be happening to *us*. (*Going up* C.)

OLIVIA. A divorce?

GEORGE. I--I imagine so.

OLIVIA. But then we could *really* get married, and we shouldn't be living in--living in--whatever we were living in before.

GEORGE (*coming down to* R. *of table* L.C.). I can't understand you, Olivia. You talk about it so calmly, as if there was nothing blameworthy in being divorced.

OLIVIA. Yes, but----

GEORGE. As if there was nothing unusual in my marrying a divorced woman.

OLIVIA. Yes, but----

GEORGE. As if there was nothing wrong in our having lived together for years without having been married.

OLIVIA (*placing her hands on table*). What seems wrong to me is that I lived for five years with a bad man whom I hated. What seems right to me is that I lived for five years with a good man whom I love.

GEORGE (*taking and patting her hands affectionately*). Yes, yes, my dear, I know. (*Drops her hands and moves to* C.) But right and wrong don't settle themselves as easily as that. We've been living together when you were Telworthy's wife. That's *wrong*.

OLIVIA. Do you mean wicked?

GEORGE. Well, no doubt the Court would consider that we acted in perfect innocence----

OLIVIA. What Court?

GEORGE. Well, you see, my dear, these things have to be done legally, of course. (***Moving to*** R. ***to settee, thinking it out***.) I believe the proper method is a nullity suit, declaring our marriage null and--er--void. It would, so to speak, wipe out these years of--er---(Moving back to C.)

OLIVIA. Wickedness?

GEORGE. Of irregular union, and-er--then----

OLIVIA. Then I could go back to Jacob.... Do you really mean that, George?

GEORGE (***uneasily***). Well, dear, you see-that's how things are--one can't get away from--er------

OLIVIA. What you feel is that Telworthy has the greater claim? You are prepared to--make way for him?

GEORGE. Both the Church and the Law would say that I had no claim at all, I'm afraid. I--I suppose I haven't.

OLIVIA. I see. (***She looks at him curiously***.) Thank you for making it so clear, George.

GEORGE. Of course, whether or not you go back to--er--Telworthy is another matter altogether. (*Crossing to fireplace*.) That would naturally be for you to decide.

OLIVIA (*cheerfully*). For me and Jacko to decide.

GEORGE. Er--Jacko?

OLIVIA. I used to call my first husband--I mean my only husband--Jacko. I didn't like the name of Jacob, and Jacko seemed to suit him somehow. (*Enjoying the joke*.) He had very long arms. (GEORGE *is very annoyed*.) Poor Jacko.

GEORGE (*annoyed*). You don't seem to realize that this is not a joke, Olivia.

OLIVIA (*still amused*). It may not be a joke, but it is funny, isn't it?

GEORGE. I must say I don't see anything funny in a tragedy that has wrecked two lives.

OLIVIA. Two? Oh, but Jacko's life isn't wrecked. It has just been miraculously restored to him. And a wife, too. There's nothing tragic for Jacko in it.

GEORGE (*stiffly*). I was referring to *our* two lives--yours and mine.

OLIVIA. Yours, George? Your life isn't wrecked. The Court will absolve you of all blame; your friends will sympathize with you, and tell you that I was a designing woman who deliberately took you in; your Aunt Julia--

GEORGE (*overwrought*). Stop it! (*Crossing over to her*.) What do you mean? Have you no heart? (OLIVIA *gives a little hurt cry*.) Do you think

I *want* to lose you, Olivia? (*Sits on her* L.) Do you think I *want* my home broken up like this? Haven't you been happy with me these last five years?

OLIVIA. Very happy.

GEORGE. Well then, how can you talk like that?

OLIVIA. But you want to send me away,

GEORGE. There you go again. I don't *want* to. I have hardly had time to realize just what it will mean to me when you go. The fact is I simply daren't realize it. I daren't think about it.

OLIVIA. Try thinking about it, George.

GEORGE. And you talk as if I *wanted* to send you away!

OLIVIA. Try thinking about it, George.

GEORGE. You don't seem to understand that I'm not *sending* you away. You simply aren't mine to keep.

OLIVIA. Whose am I?

GEORGE (*dubiously*). Your husband's. Telworthy's.

OLIVIA (*gently*). If I belong to anybody but myself, I think I belong to you.

GEORGE. Not in the eyes of the Law. Not in the eyes of the Church. Not even in the eyes of--er----

OLIVIA. The County?

GEORGE (*annoyed*). I was about to say "Heaven."

OLIVIA. Oh!

GEORGE (*rising and crossing below* OLIVIA *to* C.). That this should happen to *us*! (OLIVIA works in silence. Then she shakes out her curtains.)

OLIVIA (*looking at them*). I do hope Jacko will like these.

GEORGE (*turning and seeing curtains*). What! You----(Going up to her quickly and taking her by the hands raises her from the settee.) Olivia, Olivia, have you no heart?

OLIVIA. Ought you to talk like that to another man's wife?

GEORGE. Confound it, is this just a joke to you?

OLIVIA. You must forgive me, George; I am a little over-excited--at the thought of returning to Jacob.

GEORGE. Do you *want* to return to him?

OLIVIA. One wants to do what is right. In the eyes of--er--Heaven.

GEORGE. Seeing what sort of a man he is, I have no doubt that you could get a separation, supposing that he didn't--er--divorce you. I don't know *what* is best. I must consult my solicitor. The whole position has been sprung on us, and (*miserably sits on stool* L.C.) I don't know, I don't know. I can't take it all in. (Leaning forward and burying his face in his hands.)

OLIVIA. Wouldn't you like to consult your Aunt Julia too? She could tell you what the County--I mean what Heaven really thought about it.

GEORGE. Yes, yes. Aunt Julia has plenty of common sense. You're quite right, Olivia. This isn't a thing we can keep from the family.

OLIVIA. Do I still call her *Aunt* Julia?

(ANNE *comes in from staircase up* R. GEORGE *does not see her, but* OLIVIA *attracts his attention*.)

GEORGE (*looking up at* OLIVIA). What? What? (*Rising and crossing up to* ANNE.) Well, what is it?

ANNE. Mr. Pim says he will come down at once, sir.

GEORGE. Oh, thank you, thank you.

(OLIVIA *picks up curtains.* ANNE *goes out up staircase up* R.)

OLIVIA. George, Mr. Pim has got to know.

GEORGE. I don't see the necessity.

OLIVIA. Not even for me? When a woman suddenly hears that her long-lost husband is restored to her, don't you think she wants to ask questions? Where is he living, and how is he looking, and--

GEORGE (*very angry, going to writing-table, sits*). Of course, if you are interested in these things--

OLIVIA. How can I help being? Don't be so silly, George. (*Moves up to R. of* GEORGE *with the curtains on her arm*.) We *must* know what Jacko--

GEORGE (*annoyed*) I wish you wouldn't call him by that ridiculous name.

OLIVIA. My husband--

GEORGE (*wincing*). Yes, well--your husband?

OLIVIA. Well, we must know his plans--where we can communicate with him,
and so on.

GEORGE. I have no wish to communicate with him.

OLIVIA. I'm afraid you'll have to, dear.

GEORGE. I don't see the necessity.

OLIVIA. Well, you'll want to--to apologize to him for living with his wife for so long. (GEORGE *looks up and round at her nonplussed*). And as I belong to him, he ought to be told where he can--call for me.

GEORGE (*after a struggle and scratching his head*). You put it in a very peculiar way, but I see your point. (*With a shudder*.) Oh, the horrible publicity of it all! (*Turns away and leans on writing-table*.)

OLIVIA (going up to him and comforting him, placing her hands on his shoulders). Poor George. Dear, don't think I don't sympathize with you. I understand so exactly what you are feeling. The publicity! It's terrible.

GEORGE (*miserably and turning in his chair to her*). I want to do what's right. You believe that, don't you?

OLIVIA. Of course I do. (*Taking her hands away*.) It's only that we don't quite agree as to what is right and what is wrong.

GEORGE. It isn't a question of agreeing. Right is right, and wrong is wrong, all the world over.

OLIVIA (*with a sad little smile*). But more particularly in Buckinghamshire, I think.

GEORGE. If I only considered myself, I should say: "Let us pack this man Telworthy back to Australia. He would make no claim. He would accept money to go away and say nothing about it." If I consulted simply my own happiness, Olivia, that, is what I should say. But when I consult--er--

OLIVIA (*with great feeling*). Mine?

GEORGE. My conscience----

OLIVIA (*disappointed*). Oh!

GEORGE. Then I can't do it. (*Rises and is going up* L.) It's wrong.

OLIVIA (*making her first appeal*). Yes; but, George, don't you think I'm worth a little--

GEORGE (*turning round, seeing* DINAH *coming*). H'sh! Dinah! (Moves back to writing-table. Loudly for *DINAH'S* benefit.) Well, then I'll write to him and--Ah, Dinah, where's Aunt Julia?

DINAH (*coming in from up* L.). We've seen the pigs, and now she's discussing the Art of Landseer with Brian. (Crossing in front of writing-table to OLIVIA.) I just came to ask--

OLIVIA. Dinah, dear, bring Aunt Julia here. And Brian too. We have things we want to talk about with you all.

DINAH. Right-o! (*Moves back up* L.)

GEORGE (*outraged*). Olivia!

DINAH (*turning on terrace*). What fun!

(OLIVIA *goes to table* L.C. *and picks up her work-box. Exit* DINAH L.)

GEORGE. Olivia, you don't seriously suggest that we should discuss these things with a child like Dinah and a young man like Strange, a mere acquaintance.

OLIVIA. Dinah will have to know. I'm very fond of her, George. You can't send me away without telling Dinah. And Brian is my friend. (Moving to cabinet, puts curtains and work-box on top of cabinet.) You have your solicitor and your aunt and your conscience to consult--mayn't I even have Brian?

GEORGE (*forgetting*). I should have thought that your *husband*--

OLIVIA (*coming down to* L. *back end of settee* L.). Yes, but we don't know where Jacko is.

GEORGE. I was not referring to--er--Telworthy.

OLIVIA. Well then?

GEORGE. Oh, of course--You--naturally I--Oh, this is horrible! (Sits with his face in his hands at writing-table.)

(OLIVIA *is about to speak to him as* LADY MARDEN *enters from up* L. LADY MARDEN *looks at* GEORGE, *then moves down to centre.* DINAH *follows and comes to* L. *back end of settee.* BRIAN *follows* DINAH *and comes to back of table* L.C. OLIVIA *moves round to* L. end of settee L.)

OLIVIA (*after a pause*). George and I have had some rather bad news, Aunt Julia. We wanted your advice. Where will you sit?

LADY MARDEN. Thank you, Olivia. I can sit down by myself.

(*She does so, on lower end of settee* R., *moving cushion away*.)

OLIVIA (*to* DINAH). You sit there, my darling.

(DINAH *sits in arm-chair down* L. *and* OLIVIA *on settee* L. There is a good pause. *ALL* are looking very uncomfortable.)

LADY MARDEN. Well, what is it?

(*Another pause*. ALL *are still looking very uncomfortable*.)

Money, I suppose; nobody's safe nowadays.

(*There is another good pause*. GEORGE *looks up hopelessly at* LADY MARDEN. BRIAN *moves up inquisitively towards* GEORGE, who turns and
gradually raising his head catches sight of **BRIAN** and gives him a severe look and **BRIAN** retreats quickly to back of **L.C.** table.)

GEORGE (*signalling for help*). Olivia----

OLIVIA (*after a pause*). We've just heard that my first husband is still alive.

DINAH. Telworthy!

BRIAN. Good Lord!

LADY MARDEN. George!

DINAH (*excitedly*). And only this morning I was saying that nothing ever happened in this house! (*Rising from arm-chair and sitting to* L. *of* OLIVIA *and remorsefully to her*.) Darling, I don't mean that. Darling one!

LADY MARDEN. What does this mean, George? I leave you for ten min-utes--
barely ten minutes--to go and look at the pigs, and when I come back you tell me that Olivia is a bigamist.

(DINAH *jumps up and moves to* L. *of settee* L.)

BRIAN (*indignantly advancing towards* LADY MARDEN). I say----

OLIVIA (*restraining him*). H'sh!

BRIAN (*to* OLIVIA *and taking her hand across table* L.C.). If this is a row, I'm on your side.

LADY MARDEN. Well, George?

GEORGE (*rising and coming down to* LADY MARDEN). I'm afraid it's true, Aunt Julia. (*Taking stool from* L.C. *to* C., *sits on it*. DINAH sits in arm-chair down L.) We heard the news just before lunch--just before you came. We've only this moment had an opportunity of talking about it, of wondering what to do.

LADY MARDEN. What was his name----Tel--something----

OLIVIA. Jacob Telworthy.

LADY MARDEN (*in amazement*). So he's alive still?

GEORGE. Apparently. There seems to be no doubt about it.

LADY MARDEN (*to* OLIVIA). Didn't you *see* him die? I should always want to *see* my husband die before I married again. Not that I approve of second marriages, anyhow. I told you so at the time, George.

OLIVIA. *And* me, Aunt Julia.

LADY MARDEN. Did I? Well, I generally say what I think.

GEORGE. I ought to tell you, Aunt Julia, that no blame attaches to Olivia over this. Of that I am perfectly satisfied. It's nobody's fault, except----

LADY MARDEN. Except Telworthy's. *He* seems to have been rather careless. Well, what are you going to do about it?

GEORGE. That's just it. It's a terrible situation (With a gesture of despair.) There's bound to be so much publicity. Not only all this, but-- but Telworthy's past.

LADY MARDEN. I should have said that it was Telworthy's present which, was the trouble. Had he a past as well?

OLIVIA. He was a fraudulent company promoter. He went to prison a good deal.

(*General consternation*. BRIAN *gives a long whistle and goes up*.)

LADY MARDEN. George, you never told me this!

GEORGE. I--er----

OLIVIA. I don't see *why* he should want to talk about it.

DINAH (*indignantly rising and moving to L. end of settee* L.). What's it got to do with Olivia, anyhow? It's not *her* fault.

LADY MARDEN (*sarcastically and emphatically*). Oh, no, I daresay it's mine.

(*There is an uncomfortable pause*.)

OLIVIA (*to* GEORGE). You wanted to ask Aunt Julia what was the right thing to do.

BRIAN (*crossing down L.C. and bursting out*). Good Heavens, what is there to do except the one and only thing? (They all look at him and he becomes embarrassed and backs up stage a little.) I'm sorry. You don't want *me* to----

OLIVIA (*taking his hand across table* L.C.). *I* do, Brian.

LADY MARDEN. Well, go on, Mr. Strange. What would *you* do in George's position?

BRIAN (*crosses down to back of table* L.C.). Do? Say to the woman I loved, "You're *mine* (*bangs table with his fist*), and let this other damned fellow come and take you from me if he can!" And he couldn't--how could he?--not if the woman chose *me*.

(LADY MARDEN *gazes at* BRIAN *in amazement*, GEORGE *in anger*. OL-IVIA
presses his hand gratefully. He has said what she has been waiting--oh, so eagerly--for *GEORGE* to say. *GEORGE* rises and goes angrily up to BRIAN, *who defies him*. GEORGE *is subdued and moves helplessly up* C. *followed by* BRIAN, *who is still defiant*. DINAH *rises and runs up* L. *and round back of settee* L. *and up to left of* BRIAN and takes his arm.)

DINAH (*adoringly*). Oh, Brian! (*In a loud whisper*.) It *is* me, isn't it, and not Olivia?

BRIAN. You baby, of course!

LADY MARDEN. I'm afraid, Mr. Strange (DINAH with an exclamation of annoyance comes down to *L.* of settee L.), your morals are as peculiar as your views on Art.

BRIAN (*down to back of table* L.C.). This is not a question of morals or of art, it's a question of love.

DINAH. Hear, hear!

LADY MARDEN (*to* GEORGE). Isn't it that girl's bed-time yet?

OLIVIA (*to* DINAH *and taking her hand*). We'll let her sit up a little longer if she's good.

DINAH. I will be good, Olivia (*aggressively to* LADY MARDEN), only I thought anybody, however important a debate was, was allowed to say "Hear, hear!"

GEORGE (*coming down* C.). Really, Olivia, I really think we could discuss this better if Mr. Strange took Dinah out for a walk. Strange, If you--er----

OLIVIA. Tell them what you have settled first, George.

LADY MARDEN. Settled? What is there to be settled? It settles itself.

GEORGE (*sadly*). That's just it.

LADY MARDEN. The marriage must be annulled--is that the word, George?

GEORGE. I presume so. (*Sits on stool* C.)

LADY MARDEN. One's solicitor will know all about that, of course.

BRIAN. And when the marriage has been annulled, what then?

LADY MARDEN. Presumably Olivia will return to her husband.

BRIAN (*bitterly to* LADY MARDEN). And *that's* morality! As expounded by
Bishop Landseer!

GEORGE (*angered, rising and facing* BRIAN). I don't know what you mean by Bishop Landseer. Morality is acting in accordance with the Laws of the

Land and the Laws of the Church. I am quite prepared to believe that your creed embraces neither marriage (DINAH gives a little cry and bangs a cushion on settee angrily) nor monogamy, but my creed is different.

BRIAN (*fiercely*). My creed includes both marriage and monogamy, and monogamy means sticking to the woman you love, as long as she wants you.

LADY MARDEN (*calmly*). You suggest that George and Olivia should go on living together, although they have never been legally married. Bless the man, what do you think the County would say?

BRIAN (*scornfully*). Does it matter?

DINAH. Well, if you really want to know, the men would say, "Gad, she's a fine woman; I don't wonder he sticks to her," and the women would say, "I can't *think* what he sees in her to stick to her like that," and they'd both say, "After all, he may be a damn fool, but you can't deny he's a sportsman."

(LADY MARDEN *is very indignant*.)

GEORGE (*indignantly*). Was it for this sort of thing Olivia, that you insisted on having Dinah and Mr. Strange in here? To insult me in my own house?

LADY MARDEN. I can't think what young people are coming to nowadays.

OLIVIA. I think, dear, you and Brian had better go.

DINAH (*getting up*). We will go. (*Crossing below* OLIVIA and putting her knee on stool and looking cheekily up into *GEORGE's* face.) But I'm just going to say one thing, Uncle George. Brian and I *are* going to marry each other, and when we are married we'll stick to each other, however many of our dead husbands and wives turn up! Come on, Brian. (***She goes up*** C. and through window and goes out indignantly, followed by BRIAN R.)

(GEORGE *follows them up*.)

GEORGE. Upon my word, this is a pleasant discussion.

OLIVIA. I think the discussion is over, George. It is only a question of where I shall go, while you are bringing your--what sort of suit did you call it?

LADY MARDEN (*to* GEORGE). Nullity suit. I suppose that *is* the best thing?

GEORGE. It's horrible. (***Moving down between stool and*** LADY MARDEN.) The
awful publicity. That it should be happening to *us*, that's what I can't get over.

LADY MARDEN. I don't remember anything of the sort in the Marden Family
before, ever.

GEORGE (*absently*). Lady Fanny.

LADY MARDEN (*recollecting*). Yes, of course; but that was two hundred years ago. The standards were different then. (***Rising and going up*** C. *to* R.) Besides, it wasn't quite the same, anyhow.

GEORGE (*absently*). No, it wasn't quite the same.

LADY MARDEN (*R. of writing-table*). No. We shall all feel it. Terribly.

GEORGE (*his apology*). If there were any other way! Olivia, what *can* I do? It *is* the only way, isn't it? All that that fellow said--of course, it sounds very well--but as things are.... (*Crossing towards* OLIVIA.) *Is* there anything in marriage, or isn't there? You believe that there is, don't you? You aren't one of these Socialists. Well, then, *can* we go on living together when you're another man's wife? It isn't only what people will say, but it *is* wrong, isn't it?.... And supposing he doesn't divorce you, are we to go on living together, unmarried, for *ever*? (LADY MARDEN *turns and listens*.) Olivia, you seem to think that I'm just thinking of the publicity--what people will say. I'm not. I'm not. That comes in any way. But I want to do what's right, what's best. I don't mean what's best for us, what makes us happiest, I mean what's really best, what's rightest. What anybody else would do in my place. (OLIVIA *holds out her hands lovingly towards him*.) *I* don't know. It's so unfair. You're not my wife at all, but I want to do what's right.... (*Sits foot of table* L.C.) Oh, Olivia, Olivia, you do understand, don't you?

(*They have both forgotten* LADY MARDEN. OLIVIA has never taken her eyes
off him as he makes his last attempt to convince himself.)

OLIVIA (*almost tenderly*). So very, very well, George. Oh, I understand just what you are feeling. And oh, I do so wish that you could--(with a little sigh)--but then it wouldn't be George, not the George I married--(*with a rueful little laugh*)--or didn't quite marry.

LADY MARDEN. I must say, I think you are both talking a little wildly.

OLIVIA (*repeating it, oh, so tenderly*). Or didn't--quite--marry.

(She looks at him with all her heart in her eyes. She is giving him his last chance to say "Damn Telworthy; you're mine!" He rises and crosses to *R.* He struggles desperately with himself, turns to OLIVIA.)

GEORGE. Olivia! Olivia! My darling!

(*She rises. He crosses to her and takes her in his arms*.)

(ANNE *enters from double doors* R.)

ANNE. Mr. Pim is here, sir.

OLIVIA (*prompting him*). Mr. Pim, dear.

GEORGE (*emerging from the struggle with an effort*). Pim? Pim? Oh, ah, yes, of course. (*Crossing up to* ANNE.) Mr. Pim. (*Looking up*.) Where have you put him?

OLIVIA. I want to see Mr. Pim, too, George.

LADY MARDEN (*coming down* C. *to* R. *of table* L.C.). Who on earth is Mr. Pim?

OLIVIA. Show him in here, Anne. (GEORGE *comes back to* C.)

ANNE. Yes, madam.

(*She goes out double doors* R.)

OLIVIA. It was Mr. Pim who told us about my husband. He came across with him in the boat, and recognized him as the Telworthy he knew in Australia.

LADY MARDEN. Oh! Shall I be in the way? (*Moving down to* R.C.)

GEORGE. No, no. It doesn't matter, does it, Olivia?

OLIVIA. Please stay.

(LADY MARDEN *sits* R. *settee*.)

(ANNE *enters at double doors followed by* MR. PIM.)

ANNE. Mr. Pim.

GEORGE (*pulling himself together*). Ah, Mr. Pim! Very good of you to have come.

PIM. Oh, not at all!

GEORGE. The fact is--er--(It is too much for him; he looks despairingly at OLIVIA.)

OLIVIA. We're so sorry to trouble you, Mr. Pim. By the way, do you know Lady Marden?

PIM (*centre*). No, I haven't the honour.

GEORGE (*introducing*). My Aunt! Mr. Pim.

(MR. PIM *and* LADY MARDEN *bow to each other*.)

OLIVIA. Do come and sit down, won't you? (*Pim is moving to* L., turns and bumps into **GEORGE,** who is following him. She makes room for him on the sofa next to her.) The fact is, Mr. Pim, you gave us rather a surprise this morning, and before we had time to realize what it all meant, you had gone.

PIM. A surprise, Mrs. Marden? Dear me, not an unpleasant one, I hope?

OLIVIA. Well, rather a--surprising one. (LADY MARDEN *coughs*.)

(*Pim sits to* R. *of* OLIVIA, *who takes his hat and places it to her* L.)

GEORGE (*turns to* LADY MARDEN). Olivia, allow me a moment. Mr. Pim, you
mentioned a man called Telworthy this morning. My wife used to (LADY MARDEN *gives a pronounced cough*)--that is to say, I used to--that is, there are reasons--

OLIVIA. I think we had better be perfectly frank, George.

LADY MARDEN (*aggressively*). I am sixty-five years of age, Mr. Pim, and I can say that I've never had a moment's uneasiness by (beating her knee with her hand, stick in left hand) telling the truth.

(PIM *and* LADY MARDEN *fix each other with a look*. PIM *then looks at* OLIVIA *and* GEORGE *and leans back on settee*.)

PIM (*after a desperate effort to keep up with the conversation*). Oh!... I--er--I'm afraid I am rather at sea. Have I--er--left anything unsaid in presenting my credentials to you this morning?

GEORGE *and* OLIVIA Oh, no!

PIM. This Telworthy whom you mention--I seem to remember the name--

OLIVIA. Mr. Pim, you told us this morning of a man whom you had met on the boat, a man who had come down in the world, whom you had known in Sydney. A man called Telworthy.

PIM (*relieved*). Ah, yes, yes, of course. (*To* OLIVIA.) I did say Telworthy, didn't I? Most curious coincidence, Lady Marden. Poor man, poor man! Let me see, it must have been ten years ago--

GEORGE. Just a moment, Mr. Pim. You're quite sure that his name was Telworthy?

PIM (*to* GEORGE). Telworthy--Telworthy--didn't I say Telworthy? Yes, that was it--Telworthy. Poor fellow!

OLIVIA. I'm going to be perfectly frank with you, Mr. Pim. I feel quite sure that I can trust you.

PIM. Oh, Mrs. Marden!

OLIVIA. This man Telworthy whom you met is my husband.

PIM. Your husband! (*He looks in mild surprise at* GEORGE.) Your--er----

OLIVIA. My first husband. His death was announced six years ago. I had left him some years before that, but there seems no doubt from your story that he's still alive. His record--the country he comes from--above all, the very unusual name--Telworthy.

PIM. Telworthy--yes--certainly a most peculiar name. I remember saying so. Your first husband? Dear me! Dear me!

GEORGE. You understand, Mr. Pim, that all this is in absolute confidence.

PIM (*turning to* GEORGE). Of course, of course.

OLIVIA (*pulling his arm, trying to attract his attention*). Well, since he is my husband, we naturally want to know something about him. Where is he now, for instance?

PIM (*surprised and turning to* OLIVIA). Where is he now? But surely I told you? I told you what happened at Marseilles?

GEORGE. At Marseilles?

PIM (*to* GEORGE). Yes, yes, poor fellow, it was most unfortunate. (*To* LADY MARDEN. OLIVIA again pulls his arm, trying to attract his attention.*) You must understand, Lady Marden, that although I had met the poor fellow before in Australia, I was never in any way intimate----

GEORGE (*thumping the desk*). Where is he *now*, that's what we want to know?

(MR. PIM *turns to him with a start*.)

OLIVIA. Please, Mr. Pim!

PIM (*to* OLIVIA). Where is he now? But--but didn't I tell you of the curious fatality at Marseilles--poor fellow--the fish-bone?

ALL. Fish-bone?

PIM. Yes, yes, a herring, I understand.

OLIVIA (*becoming hysterical*). Do you mean he's dead?

PIM. Dead--of course he's dead. He's been dead----

OLIVIA (*laughing hysterically*). Oh, Mr. Pim, you--oh, what a husband to have--oh, I----(*But that is all she can say for the moment*.)

LADY MARDEN. Pull yourself together, Olivia. (*To* PIM.) So he really is dead this time?

PIM. Oh, undoubtedly, undoubtedly. A fish-bone lodged in his throat.

(LADY MARDEN *retreats to settee* R. *again*.)

GEORGE (*moving up* C. *to* L. *window, trying to realize it*). Dead! Dead!

PIM (*rising and turning to* OLIVIA, *alarmed at her hysteria*). Oh, but, Mrs. Marden!

OLIVIA. I think you must excuse me, Mr. Pim. (*Crossing to* C.) But a herring! There's something about a herring----

(GEORGE *comes quickly to her, very concerned*.)

(PIM *is also very concerned*.)

(*Turning to* GEORGE.) Oh, George! (Shaking her head in a weak state of laughter, turns to *R.* and is about to hurry out of the room towards staircase R.)

QUICK CURTAIN.

ACT III

SCENE.-- *The same and furniture exactly as in* ACT II.

(MR. PIM *is below settee* L. standing in same position as at the end
of *ACT II. GEORGE MARDEN* is in centre of stage and *LADY MARDEN* is at
foot of staircase. Their altitude is the same as at the end of ACT II,
and all are concerned about OLIVIA'S *hysteria*.)

GEORGE. Dead! Dead!

PIM. Oh dear! Oh dear! I'm afraid I broke the news rather hastily. The
double shock of losing one husband and being restored to another--

LADY MARDEN (*coming to* GEORGE). A dispensation of Providence,
George.
One can regard it in no other light. (*Moves to* R. *of writing-table*.)

GEORGE (*coming to* PIM). Yes! Yes! Well, I'm much obliged to you, Mr.
Pim, for having come down to us this afternoon, and you understand that
your news, though tardy, has been very welcome. *De Mortuis*, and so
forth.

(LADY MARDEN *crosses at back of writing-table to* L.)

PIM (*sadly repeating*). *De Mortuis--*

GEORGE (*shaking hands--anxious to get rid of him*). Well, good-bye, and again our thanks.

(*Crosses below and to* L. *of* PIM *and rings bell below fireplace*.)

PIM (*crossing to centre*). Not at all. I shouldn't have broken the news so hastily. (*Catches sight of* LADY MARDEN *up* L., and with a profound bow.) Good-bye, Lady Marden.

LADY MARDEN (*equally profound*). Good-bye, Mr. Pim.

PIM. I'm afraid I broke the news too hastily. (*Goes to table* B.C. and takes up *GEORGE'S* cap in mistake for his hat and is moving towards double-doors when *GEORGE,* noting this, picks up *PIM'S* hat from L. *of stage where it has been left from previous* ACT, and crosses with it to PIM.)

GEORGE. Mr. Pim, excuse me, but I think this is yours.

PIM (*he takes it and looks at it closely, comparing it with the cap*). This isn't my hat at all. (*Puts* GEORGE'S *cap down on table again*.)

No, that isn't my hat. (*Takes his own hat from* GEORGE.) This is my hat. Good-bye! (*Shakes hands*.) Thank you so much. (Looking at cap on table.) Oh, no! Oh, no! (*Moves nearer to door* R.) Telworthy... I *think* that was the name.

(*Exit doors* R.)

(LADY MARDEN, *annoyed at* PIM'S *stupidity, comes down to* L. *of* GEORGE.)

GEORGE (*turning to* LADY MARDEN *and with a sigh of thankfulness*). Well, this is wonderful news, Aunt Julia.

LADY MARDEN. Most providential. Well, I must be getting along now, George. Say good-bye to Olivia for me.

GEORGE (*crossing towards double-doors as if to open them*). Good-bye, Aunt Julia.

LADY MARDEN. No! No! I'll go this way--(*going up to* L. of writing-table)--and get Olivia out more, George. I don't like these hysterics. (*Banging writing-table*.) You want to be firmer with her.

GEORGE. Yes! Yes! Good-bye.

LADY MARDEN (*going off up* L.). Good-bye.

GEORGE (*back again down centre and with great thankfulness*). Dead! Dead! (*Moves down to below settee* L.)

(OLIVIA *enters from staircase, watching him and coming quietly to* C.)

GEORGE (*approaching her enthusiastically*). Olivia! Olivia! (Is about to embrace her, but she restrains him.)

OLIVIA (*drawing herself up*). Mrs. Telworthy!

GEORGE (*taken aback*). What? Olivia! I--I don't understand.

OLIVIA. Well, darling, if my husband only died at Marseilles a few days ago----

GEORGE (*scratching his head*). Yes, I see--I see. Well, we can soon put that right. (*Moving to* L.) A registry office in London. Better go up this afternoon. We can't do these things too quickly--we can stay at an hotel.

OLIVIA (*pointedly*). You and Mrs. Telworthy! (Moves slowly round back of settee L.)

(GEORGE *moves to centre*.)

GEORGE (*nonplussed*). Oh--er--yes--yes--perhaps I'd better stay at my Club--yes! It will be a bit awkward at first. (*With a sigh of relief*.) However, nobody need know, and how much better than what we feared!

(OLIVIA *comes down to below settee* L.)

GEORGE (*advancing to embrace her*). Olivia! Olivia!

(*She repulses him and he crosses to her* L.)

OLIVIA. Mrs. Telworthy!

GEORGE. Yes--yes, I know, but why do you keep on saying it? What's the matter with you? You're so strange to-day. You're not like the Olivia I know.

OLIVIA (*sits on settee to* R.). Perhaps you don't know me so very well, after all.

GEORGE (*sitting--affectionately to her* L.). Oh, that's nonsense--old girl. You're just my Olivia. Now we can get married again quietly and nobody will be any the worse.

OLIVIA. Married again! Oh, I see, you want me to marry you at a registry office to-morrow?

GEORGE. If we can arrange it by then. (*Rising and crossing below* OLIVIA *to centre*.) I don't know how long these things take, but I should imagine there would be no difficulty.

OLIVIA. Oh, no, I think that part of it ought to be quite *easy*. But-- (*She hesitates*.)

GEORGE. But what?

OLIVIA. Well, if you want to marry me to-morrow, George, oughtn't you to propose to me first?

GEORGE (*amazed*). Propose?

OLIVIA. Yes. It is usual, isn't it, to propose to a person before you marry her? And--and we want to do the usual thing, don't we?

GEORGE (*upset*). But you--I mean we--

OLIVIA. You are George Marden, I am Olivia Telworthy, you are attracted by me and think I would make you a good wife, and you want to marry me--very well, then, naturally you propose to me first.

GEORGE (falling into the humour of it, as he thinks, and with a hearty laugh moves to below stool L.C.). The baby! Did she want to be proposed to all over again?

OLIVIA (*coyly*). Well, she did rather.

GEORGE (rather fancying himself as an actor, he adopts what he considers to be an appropriate attitude). She shall then. Er--ah, Mrs. Telworthy, I have long admired you in silence, and the time has now come to put my admiration into words (*but apparently he finds a difficulty*)--er--er--

OLIVIA (looking up at him quizzically and prompting him into words; repeating). I--I--(*Looking down coyly*.) Oh, Mr. Marden!

(GEORGE *roars with laughter and crosses to centre*.)

GEORGE (*returning to her*). Olivia--er--may I call you Olivia?

OLIVIA. Yes, George.

(OLIVIA *puts out her hand and* GEORGE *notices it*.)

GEORGE. I beg your pardon! Oh, I see. (Taking her hand in his he gives it a good slap and she winces.) Olivia, I--(*Hesitates*.)

OLIVIA. I don't want to interrupt, but oughtn't you to be on your knees? It is--usual, I believe. GEORGE. Really, Olivia, you must allow me to manage my own proposal in my own way.

OLIVIA (*meekly--and resuming her coyness*). I'm sorry. Do go on.

GEORGE. Well--er--confound it, Olivia, I love you. Will you marry me?

OLIVIA. Thank you, George, I will think it over.

GEORGE (*laughing*). Silly girl. (Pats her on the shoulder and crosses to R.) Well, then, to-morrow morning. No wedding cake, I'm afraid, Olivia. (*He laughs again and moves up centre*.) But we'll go and have a good lunch somewhere.

OLIVIA. I will think it over, George.

GEORGE (*good-humouredly and coming down to back of settee to her* R.). Well, give me a kiss while you're thinking.

OLIVIA. I'm afraid you mustn't kiss me until we are actually engaged.

GEORGE (*laughing uneasily, and sitting and leaning over on table* L.C. *towards* OLIVIA). Oh, we needn't take it as seriously as all that.

OLIVIA. But a woman must take a proposal seriously.

GEORGE (*a little alarmed at last*). What do you mean?

OLIVIA. Well, what I mean is that the whole question--(with a sly look at GEORGE)--as I heard somebody say once, demands much more anxious thought than either of us has given it. These hasty marriages----

GEORGE (*rising and crossing at back of* OLIVIA *round settee and to* L. *of* OLIVIA). Hasty!

OLIVIA. Well, you've only just proposed to me, and you want me to marry you to-morrow.

GEORGE. Now you're talking perfect nonsense, Olivia. You know quite well that our case is utterly different from--well--from any other.

OLIVIA. All the same, one must ask oneself questions. With a young girl like--well, with a young girl--love may well seem to be all that matters.

But with a woman of my age it is different. I have to ask myself whether you can afford to support a wife.

GEORGE. You know perfectly well that I can afford to support a wife as my wife should be supported.

OLIVIA. Oh, I am glad. Then your income--you are not really worried about that at all?

GEORGE (*stiffly*). You know perfectly well what my income is. I see no reason for anxiety, in the future.

OLIVIA. Ah, very well, then we needn't think about it any more.

GEORGE. You know I can't make out what you're up to. (**Sits to her** L. **on settee**.) Don't you want to get married--to--er--legalize this extraordinary situation in which we are placed?

OLIVIA. I must consider the whole question very carefully. I can't just jump at the very first offer I have had since my husband died. (Rising and crossing to centre.)

GEORGE. Oh, so I'm under consideration, eh?

OLIVIA (**moving up** R.C.). Every suitor is.

GEORGE. Oh, very well, go on! Go on!

OLIVIA. Well then, there's your niece. You have a niece living with you. Of course Dinah is a delightful girl, but one doesn't like marrying into a household where there's another grown-up woman. But perhaps she will be getting married herself soon.

GEORGE. I see no prospect of it.

OLIVIA. It would make it so much easier, George, if she did.

GEORGE (*rising*). Is this a threat, Olivia? (***Crossing up to*** OLIVIA.)
Are you telling me that if I do not allow young Strange to marry Dinah,
you will not marry me?

OLIVIA. A threat? Oh, no, George. But I was just wondering if you love me
as much as Brian loves Dinah. You do love me?

GEORGE (*from his heart*). Of course I do, old girl.

OLIVIA. You're sure it's not just my pretty face that attracts you. Love
which is based upon mere outward appearances cannot result in lasting
happiness--as one of our thinkers has observed. (***Moving down to settee***
R.)

GEORGE. Why should you doubt my love? You can't pretend that we haven't
been happy together. (OLIVIA *sits on settee* R.) I've--(taking a chair
from *L.* of table *R.C.* brings it down to *L.* of OLIVIA) I've been a
good pal to you, eh? We--we suit each other, old girl.

OLIVIA. Do we?

GEORGE (*sitting*). Well, of course we do.

OLIVIA. I wonder. When two people of our age think of getting married,
one wants to be quite sure that there is real community of ideas between
them. Supposing that after we have been married some years we found
ourselves getting estranged from each other upon such questions as
Dinah's future, or the comparatively trivial matter like the right colour
for a curtain, or the advice to be given to a friend who had innocently

contracted a bigamous marriage. Think how bitterly we should regret our hasty plunge into a matrimony which was no true partnership, whether of tastes or ideas or even of consciences. (*With a sigh*.) Ah me!

GEORGE (*turning to her quickly*). Unfortunately for your argument, Olivia, I can answer you out of your own mouth. You seem to have-- (*laughing*)--forgotten what you said this morning in the case of--er-- young Strange.

OLIVIA (*with exaggerated reproach*). Oh, but is it quite fair, George, to drag up *what was said this morning*?

GEORGE (*enjoying his apparent success*). Ha ha! You've brought it on yourself.

OLIVIA. I?... Well, and what did I say this morning?

GEORGE. You said that it was quite enough that Strange was n gentleman and in love with Dinah for me to let them marry each other.

OLIVIA. Oh! But is that enough, George?

GEORGE (*triumphantly*). Well, you said so.

OLIVIA (*meekly*). Well, George, if you think so too, I'm quite willing to risk it.

GEORGE (*kindly, rising and putting back chair up* R.C.). Ha ha, my dear! You see!

OLIVIA. Then you *do* think it's enough?

GEORGE. I--er--yes, yes, I--I think so.

OLIVIA (rising and going to him and putting her hands on his shoulders). My darling one! How jolly! Then we can have a double wedding.

GEORGE (*astonished*). A double one!

OLIVIA. Yes, you and me, Brian and Dinah.

GEORGE (*firmly, and taking her hands from his shoulders*). Now look here, Olivia, understand once and for all, I am not to be blackmailed into giving my consent to Dinah's engagement. Neither blackmailed nor tricked. (*Crossing to* L. *below settee*.) Our marriage has nothing whatever to do with Dinah's.

OLIVIA. No, dear, I quite understand. They may take place about the same time, but they have nothing whatever to do with each other.

GEORGE (*sits on foot of table* L.C.). I see no prospect of Dinah's marriage taking place for many years.

OLIVIA. No, dear, that was what I said.

GEORGE (*not understanding for the moment*). You said----? I see. (*Turning and facing her*.) Now look here, Olivia, let us have this perfectly clear. You apparently insist on treating my--er--proposal as serious.

OLIVIA (*mock surprise*). But isn't it? Have you been trifling with me?

GEORGE. You know perfectly well what I mean. You treat it as an ordinary proposal for a man to a woman who have never been anything to each other before. Very well then, will you kindly tell me what you propose to do if you decide to--ah--accept me? You do not suggest that we should go on living together--unmarried?

OLIVIA (*shocked*). Of course not, George!! What would--(pausing for additional explanation)--the County--I mean Heaven--I mean the Law--I mean--of course not. Besides, it's so unnecessary. If I decide to accept you, of *course* I shall marry you.

GEORGE. Quite so. And if you--ah--decide to refuse me, what will you do?

OLIVIA. Nothing.

GEORGE. Meaning by that?

OLIVIA. Just that, George. I shall stay here--just as before.

(GEORGE *rises and approaches her, about to expostulate*.)

I like this house. (*Crossing below* GEORGE, looking about the room to below settee L.) It wants a little redecorating, but I do like it, George... Yes, I shall be perfectly happy here! (*Sits on settee*.)

GEORGE. I see. You will continue to live down here--in spite of what you said just now about the--the immorality of it.

OLIVIA (*surprised*). But what is there immoral in a widow living alone in a big country house--with perhaps the niece of a dear friend of hers--staying with her to keep her company.

GEORGE (*sarcastic*). Oh, and pray what shall I be doing when you've so very kindly taken possession of my house for me?

OLIVIA. You! Oh, I can't *think*! Travelling, I expect.

GEORGE (*indignant and advancing to her*). Thank you! And suppose I refuse to be turned out of my own house?

OLIVIA. Then, seeing that we can't both be in it, it looks as though you'd have to turn me out. (*To herself.*) There must be legal ways of doing these things. You'd have to consult your solicitor again.

GEORGE. Legal ways?

OLIVIA. Well, you couldn't just throw me out, could you? You'd have to get an injunction against me--

(GEORGE, *very annoyed, turns away.*)

--or prosecute me for trespass--or something. Of course I shouldn't go if I could help it, I like the house so much.... It would make an awfully unusual case, wouldn't it? The papers would be full of it.

GEORGE. The papers!

OLIVIA (*calling as paper boy*). Extra special! Widow of well-known ex-convict takes possession of J.P.'s house! Special! Special!

GEORGE (*angrily*). I've had enough of this. (*Coming to table* L.C. and speaking across.) Do you mean all this nonsense?

OLIVIA. Well, what I *do* mean *is*, that I am in no hurry to go up to London and get married. I love the country just now, and--(with a sigh)--after this morning, I'm--rather tired of husbands.

GEORGE (*in a rage*). I've never heard so much--damned (*bangs table*) ... nonsense in my life. *I will leave you to come back to your senses.*

(*He goes out, up staircase up* R.)

(OLIVIA *rises and crosses to centre, watching* GEORGE off. She kisses her hands to him, then turning to *L.* sees curtains and work-box and extending her arms in ecstasy goes to cabinet, takes them up and comes down *L. OLIVIA* sits on settee with curtains in her lap and places the work-box to her *L.* on settee, and as she does so *MR. PIM* enters from up *R.* through windows and coming to *R.* of writing-table taps it with his umbrella to attract *OLIVIA'S* attention. She turns and sees him. He looks nervously round at staircase *R.* fearing the return of GEORGE.)

PIM (*in a whisper*). Er--may I come in, Mrs. Marden?

OLIVIA (*in surprise*). Mr. Pim!

PIM (*anxiously and again looking round at staircase*). Mr. Marden is-- er--not here?

OLIVIA (*getting up*). No! Do you want to see him? I will----

PIM (*another look round at staircase and moving down centre*). No, no, no! Not for the world. There is no immediate danger of his returning, Mrs. Marden?

OLIVIA (*surprised*). No, I don't think so, Mr. Pim. (Puts down curtains). But... what is it? You----

PIM. I took the liberty of returning by the window in the hope of finding you alone.

OLIVIA (*sitting again*). Yes?

PIM (*still rather nervous and throwing up his arms in distress*). Mr. Marden will be so angry with me, and very rightly. Oh, I blame myself. I blame myself entirely. I don't know how I can have been so stupid. (Sits on stool *L.C.* very concerned).

OLIVIA. What is it, Mr. Pim? My first husband hasn't come to life again, has he?

PIM. No! No! No! (*Looking round to* R. and speaking very mysteriously across table L.C.) The fact is--his name was Pelwittle.

OLIVIA (*at a loss*). Whose? My husband's?

PIM. Yes, yes. Henry Pelwittle, poor fellow.

OLIVIA. But *my* husband's name was Telworthy.

PIM. No! Oh dear, no! Pelwittle. (*Firmly*.) It came back to me suddenly just as I reached the gate--Henry Pelwittle, poor fellow.

OLIVIA. But really, Mr. Pim, I ought to know.

PIM. No! No! Pelwittle.

OLIVIA. But who is Pelwittle?

PIM (*in surprise at her stupidity*). The man I told you about, who met with the sad fatality at Marseilles. Henry Pelwittle.... (With hand on chin, thinking deeply.) Or was it *Ernest*? No! *Henry* Pelwittle, poor fellow.

OLIVIA (*indignantly*). But, Mr. Pim, you said his name was Telworthy. How could you?

PIM. Oh, I blame myself, I blame myself entirely.

OLIVIA. But how could you *think* of a name like Telworthy if it wasn't Telworthy?

PIM (*eagerly*). Ah, ah, that is the really interesting thing about the whole matter.

OLIVIA (*reproachfully*). Yes, Mr. Pim, all your visits here to-day have been very interesting.

PIM. Oh, very interesting, very interesting, You see, Mrs. Marden, when I made my first appearance here this morning I was received by--Miss Diana, who----

OLIVIA. Dinah!

PIM. I beg your pardon?

OLIVIA. Dinah. Her name is Dinah!

PIM (*pauses*). You're quite right. Dinah--oh yes. Miss Dinah, yes. She was in--er--rather a communicative mood, and I suppose by way of passing the time she mentioned that before your marriage--to Mr. Marden you had been a Mrs.--er----

OLIVIA. Telworthy.

PIM. Telworthy, yes, of course. She also mentioned Australia. Now by some curious process of the brain--which strikes me as decidedly curious--when

I was trying to recollect--the name of the poor fellow on the boat, whom you will remember I had also met in Australia, the fact that this other name was also stored in my memory, a name equally peculiar--this fact I say----

OLIVIA (*seeing that the sentence is rapidly going to pieces*). Yes, I quite understand.

PIM. I blame myself, I blame myself entirely.

OLIVIA. Oh, you mustn't do that, Mr. Pim.

PIM. Oh, but, Mrs. Marden, can you forgive me for the needless distress I have caused you to-day?

OLIVIA. Oh, you mustn't worry about that, please.

PIM. And you will tell your husband--you'll break the news to him?

OLIVIA (*amazed*). Oh, yes! I'll break the *news* to him.

PIM (*rising and holding out his hand*). Well then, I think before he comes back I will say good-bye and--er----

OLIVIA (*rising*). Just a moment, Mr. Pim. Let us have it quite clear this time. You never knew my husband Jacob Telworthy?

PIM. No!

OLIVIA. You never met him in Australia?

PIM. No!

OLIVIA. You never saw him on the boat?

PIM. No!

OLIVIA. And nothing *whatever happened to him at Marseilles?*

PIM. No!

OLIVIA. Is that right?

PIM (*hesitating and thinking it out very deeply*). I think so.

OLIVIA. Very well, then, since his death was announced in Australia six years ago, he is presumably still dead?

PIM. Undoubtedly.

OLIVIA (*holding out her hand with a charming smile*). Then good-bye, Mr. Pim, and thank you so much for--for all your trouble.

PIM. Not at all, Mrs. Marden. I blame myself, I blame myself entirely.

OLIVIA. Oh! You mustn't do that.

(*Going up centre* PIM *meets* DINAH, who enters from the window up L., crosses at back of writing-table and comes down R. of him).

(DINAH is followed by BRIAN, who is on her R.).

DINAH. Hullo, there's Mr. Pim. (*To* BRIAN.)

PIM (*nervously looking at the door in case* MR. MARDEN should come in). Yes, yes I--er--

DINAH. Oh, Mr. Pim, you mustn't run away without even saying how-do-you-do! Are you staying to tea?

PIM (*looking off at staircase nervously*). I'm afraid I--

OLIVIA. Mr. Pim has to hurry away, Dinah. You mustn't keep him.

DINAH. Well, but you'll come back again?

PIM. I fear that I am only a passer-by, Miss--er--Dinah.

OLIVIA. You can take Mr. Pim as far as the gate.

PIM (*gratefully to* OLIVIA). Thank you. (With nervous look at staircase R., he edges towards the windows.) If you would be so kind, Miss Dinah--.

DINAH (*taking his arm*). Come along then, Mr. Pim.

BRIAN. I'll catch you up.

DINAH (*taking him up L.*). I want to hear all about your first wife.

PIM. Oh, but I haven't got a first wife.

DINAH. You haven't really told me anything yet.

(*They go off up L.*)

BRIAN. I'll catch you up.

(OLIVIA *resumes her work, and* BRIAN crosses down to foot of table L.C., and sits on it.)

BRIAN (*awkwardly*). I just wanted to say, if you don't think it cheek, that I'm--I'm on your side, if I may be and if I can help you at all, I shall be very proud of being allowed to.

OLIVIA (*looking up at him and taking his hand*). Brian, you dear, that's sweet of you. But it's quite all right now, you know.

BRIAN. What?

OLIVIA. Yes, that's what Mr. Pim came back to say. He'd made a mistake about the name--

BRIAN (*rising*). Good Lord!

OLIVIA (*smiling*). George is the only husband I have.

BRIAN (*surprised*). What? You mean that the whole thing that Pim--

OLIVIA (*repeating*). The whole thing.

BRIAN (crossing up to window R. and shouting off to L. and with conviction). Silly ass!

OLIVIA (*kindly*). Oh, no, no, I'm sure he didn't mean to be. (After a pause.) Brian, do you know anything about the law?

BRIAN (*coming down* C.). The law? I'm afraid not. I hate the law. Why? (*Sits at foot of table* L.C.)

OLIVIA. Well, I was just wondering. Suppose that George and I had accidentally married each other a second time thinking that the first marriage wasn't quite right, and then we found the first marriage was all right--well----

BRIAN. What on earth do you mean?

OLIVIA. Well, what I mean is that there's nothing wrong in marrying the same person twice?

BRIAN (*rising and moving to centre, thinking it out*). Oh, no. A hundred times if you like, I should think.

OLIVIA. Oh!

BRIAN. After all, in France they always go through it twice, don't they? Once before the Mayor or somebody, and once in church.

OLIVIA. Of course they do! How silly of me. You know, that's a very good idea. They ought to do that more in England.

BRIAN. Well, once will be enough for Dinah and me, if you can work it. (*Anxiously*.) D'you think there's any chance, Olivia?

OLIVIA (*smiling*). Every chance, dear.

BRIAN (*coming to above table* L.C.). I say, do you really? Have you squared him? I mean has he----

(GEORGE *is heard humming the tune of "Pop goes the weasel" off* R.)

OLIVIA. You go and catch them up now. We'll talk about it later on.

BRIAN. Bless you. Right-o!

(*Going up* L. *and off up* L.)

(*As he goes out by the windows,* GEORGE *comes in at the doors* R. GEORGE *stands* R.C., *and then turns to* OLIVIA, who is absorbed in her curtain. He walks up and down the room, fidgeting with things, waiting for her to speak. As she says nothing, he begins to talk himself, but in an obviously unconcerned way. There is a pause after each answer of hers, before he gets out his next remark.)

GEORGE (*casually*). Good-looking fellow, Strange. What?

OLIVIA (*equally casually*). Brian, yes, isn't he? And such a nice boy.

GEORGE. Yes, yes! (Catching sight of curtain she is sewing. Hums the tune of "Pop goes the weasel"--crossing down *R.* to piano, plays a few notes of "Pop goes the weasel" with one finger.) Got fifty pounds for a picture the other day, didn't he? (*Moving up stage a little*.)

OLIVIA. Ah, yes! Of course he has only just begun----

GEORGE. The critics think well of him, (*Slight pause*.) What?

(*Up C. by chair front of writing-table*.)

OLIVIA. They all say he has genius. Oh, I don't think there's any doubt about it. (*Pause*.)

(GEORGE *left of writing-table*.)

GEORGE. No, no! (*Slight pause, and he sings again*.) Of course I don't profess to know anything about painting, myself.

OLIVIA. You've never had time to take it up, dear.

GEORGE (*coming down* L. *a little*.) No! No! Of course I know what I like. Can't say I see much in this new-fangled stuff. If a man can paint, why can't he paint like--like Rubens, or--or Reynolds, or----

OLIVIA. I suppose we all have our own styles. Brian will be finding his, directly. Of course, he's only just beginning. (*Pause*.)

GEORGE (*crossing up centre*). Yes, yes. But the critics think a lot of him, what?

OLIVIA. Oh, yes.

GEORGE. Yes! H'm! (*Pause*.) Good-looking fellow.

(*There is rather a longer silence this time.* GEORGE coming round back of settee L. continues to hope that he is appearing casual and unconcerned--he stands looking at **OLIVIA'S** work for a moment.)

GEORGE (*down* L.). Nearly finished 'em?

OLIVIA. Very nearly. (Smiling to herself, turns away to R., pretending to look for scissors.) Have you seen my scissors anywhere?

GEORGE (*looking round*). Scissors?

OLIVIA (*turns to* L. *and finds them in her work-box*). It's all right, here they are----

GEORGE (*down* L. *below chair facing* OLIVIA). Where are you thinking of hanging 'em?

OLIVIA (*as if really wondering*). I don't quite know.... I **had** thought of this room, but--I'm not quite sure.

GEORGE (*crossing below* OLIVIA *to centre*). Ah! Yes! Brighten the room up a bit.

OLIVIA. Yes.

GEORGE (*walking up centre a little towards windows*). H'm, yes----They are a bit faded.

OLIVIA (*shaking out hers, and looking at them critically*). You know, sometimes I think I love them, and sometimes I'm not quite sure.

GEORGE. Best way is to hang 'em up and see how you like 'em. Always take 'em down again.

OLIVIA. Oh, that's a good idea, George.

GEORGE. Best way.

OLIVIA. Yes.... I think we might try that--(looking round at settee and carpets, etc.)--the only thing is--(*She hesitates*.)

GEORGE. What?

OLIVIA. Well, the carpets and the chair-covers and the cushions and things--

GEORGE. Well, what about 'em?

OLIVIA. Well, if we had new curtains--

GEORGE. You'd want a new carpet, eh?

OLIVIA (*doubtfully*). Well, *new chair-covers, anyhow.*

GEORGE. H'm!... Well, why not?

OLIVIA. Oh, but--

GEORGE (*with an awkward laugh*). We're not so hard up as all that, you know.

OLIVIA (*quickly*). No, I don't suppose we are really--

GEORGE. No, no, no, yes--I mean no.

OLIVIA (*thoughtfully*). I suppose it would mean that I should have to go up to London to choose them. You know, that's rather a nuisance.

GEORGE (*extremely casual and moving towards* OLIVIA). Oh, I don't know.
We might go up together one day.

OLIVIA. Well, of course if we *were* up--for anything else--

GEORGE (*moving away dubiously*). Yes, yes! That's what I meant.

(*There is another silence*. GEORGE is wondering whether to come to closer quarters with the great question.)

OLIVIA. Oh, by the way, George--

GEORGE. Yes?

OLIVIA (*innocently*). I told Brian, and of course he'll tell Dinah, that Mr. Pim had made a mistake about the name.

GEORGE (*astonished, moving towards* OLIVIA). Mistake about the name?

OLIVIA. Yes--I told Brian that the whole thing was a mistake, I thought that was the simplest way.

GEORGE. Olivia--(*crossing below and to her* L.)--then you mean that Brian and Dinah think that--that we have been married all the time?

OLIVIA. Yes.

GEORGE (*coming closer to her*). Olivia, does that mean that you are thinking of marrying me?

OLIVIA. At your old registry office?

GEORGE (*eagerly*). Yes!

OLIVIA. To-morrow?

GEORGE. Yes.

OLIVIA. Do you want me to very much?

GEORGE. My darling, you know I do.

OLIVIA. We should have to keep it very quiet, George.

GEORGE. Well, of course--(*sitting to her* L.)--nobody need know. We don't want anybody to know. And now that you've put Brian and Dinah off the scent, by telling them that--(*he breaks off and says admiringly*)-- that was very clever of you, Olivia. I should never have thought of that.

OLIVIA (*innocently*). George--you don't think it was **wrong**, do you?

GEORGE (*his verdict, taking her hands and patting them*). An innocent deception... perfectly harmless.

OLIVIA. Yes, dear, that was what I thought about--about--(*laughing to herself*) what I was doing.

GEORGE. Then you will come up to London to-morrow?

(*She nods*.)

And if we should see a carpet or anything else we want----

OLIVIA. Oh, George!

GEORGE (*beaming, rising and backing away to* L. *a little*). And lunch at the Carlton, what?

OLIVIA (*nodding eagerly*). Oh!

GEORGE. And--and a bit of a honeymoon in Paris?

OLIVIA. Oh, what fun!

GEORGE (*hungrily*). Give me a kiss, old girl.

OLIVIA (*lovingly*). George!

(She holds up her cheek to him. He kisses it, and then suddenly takes her in his arms.)

GEORGE. Don't ever leave me, old girl.

OLIVIA (*affectionately*). Don't ever send me away, old boy.

GEORGE (*fervently*). I won't. (*Awkwardly*.) I--I don't think I should have really, you know. I--I----

(DINAH *enters from up* L. and crosses at back of writing-table and round down *R. BRIAN* follows her.)

DINAH (*seeing the embrace, surprised*). Oo--I say!

(GEORGE *looks and feels rather a fool*.)

GEORGE. Hallo!

(OLIVIA *sits, resumes sewing*.)

DINAH (*coming down centre and going below settee* L., impetuously to him). Give me one, too, George. Brian won't mind.

GEORGE (*formally, but enjoying it*). Do you mind, Mr. Strange?

BRIAN (*a little uncomfortable*). Oh, I say, sir----

GEORGE. We'll risk it, Dinah. (*He kisses her*.)

DINAH (*triumphantly to* BRIAN *and standing above* GEORGE). Did you notice that one? That wasn't just an ordinary affectionate kiss. That was a special "bless you my children" one. (*To* GEORGE.) Wasn't it?

OLIVIA. You do talk nonsense, darling.

DINAH (*crossing quickly below and to* R. *of* BRIAN). Well, I'm so happy now that Pim has relented about your first husband--(GEORGE *catches* OLIVIA'S eye and smiles; she smiles back; but they are different smiles.)

GEORGE (*the actor*). Yes, yes, stupid fellow, Pim, what?

BRIAN. Yes. Absolute idiot, I think!

DINAH. And now that George has relented about--(with a significant look at BRIAN)--*my* first husband----

GEORGE. Here, you get on much too quickly. (*Crossing below* OLIVIA *to* BRIAN.) So you want to marry my Dinah, eh?

BRIAN (*with a smile*). Well, I do rather, sir.

GEORGE (*to* BRIAN). Well, you'd better have a talk with me about it--er--(*with a sly look at* OLIVIA)--Brian.

BRIAN. Thank you very much, sir.

(GEORGE *goes up and* BRIAN, *imitating his walk, accompanies him*.)

GEORGE. Well, come along then. (BRIAN *looks at his watch*.) I am going up to town after tea, so we'd better----

DINAH (*moving up to* R. *of* BRIAN). I say, are you going to London?

GEORGE (*with a sly look at* OLIVIA). Yes, a little business.

DINAH (*cheekily*). Eh?

GEORGE. Never you mind, young woman. (*To* BRIAN.) Come along, we'll stroll down and look at the pigs.

BRIAN. Right-o!

(*They are going off to* L. *when* OLIVIA *calls*.)

OLIVIA. George, don't go too far away; I may want you.

GEORGE. All right! I'll be out on the terrace. Give me a shout if you want me.

(GEORGE *and* BRIAN *go off at windows up* L.)

(DINAH *follows up* R. *and watches them off*.)

DINAH (*watching them off*). Brian and George always discuss me in front of the pigs. So tactless of them. I say, are you going to London, too, darling? (*Coming down to table* L.C.)

OLIVIA. To-morrow----(*Rising and shaking out curtains*.)

DINAH. What are you going to do in London?

OLIVIA. Oh, shopping and--one or two little things.

DINAH. With George?

OLIVIA. Yes. (*Crossing up centre below* DINAH *with curtains*.)

DINAH (*sits on table* L.C.). I say, wasn't it lovely about Pim?

OLIVIA. Lovely?

DINAH. Yes, he told me all about it. Making such a hash of things, I mean.

OLIVIA (*innocently*). Did he make a hash of things?

DINAH. Well, I mean keeping on coming like that. And if you look at it all round--well, for all he had to say, he needn't have come at all.

OLIVIA. Well, I don't think I should put it quite like that, Dinah.

DINAH (*referring to curtains*). I say, aren't they jolly?

OLIVIA. I'm so glad everybody likes them. Tell George I'm ready, dear.

DINAH. I say, is *he* going to put them up for you?

OLIVIA. Well, I thought perhaps he could reach better.

DINAH. All right, I'll tell him. (*Crossing up* L. on to terrace and calling off.) George! (*Returning to back* L. *end of writing-table*.) Brian is just telling George about the five shillings he has in the Post Office--(*crossing up* L. *on to terrace again and calling off*.) George!!

GEORGE (*from off* L.). Coming!

DINAH (*playfully coming down centre, imitating a fairy's footsteps*). Slow music while the curtains go up. (Sits at piano and plays "As I passed by your Window.")

(*GEORGE enters from up* L., *followed by* BRIAN.)

GEORGE (*to* OLIVIA). What is it, darling?

OLIVIA. I wish you'd help me to put up these curtains?

GEORGE. Of course, dear. I'd better get the library steps. (Crosses to doors R. and exits.)

(BRIAN goes quickly to OLIVIA and gratefully kisses her hand, then comes down to DINAH and bows to her.)

BRIAN. Madam! I have the honour to inform you that hence-forward you are at liberty to regard me as your affianced husband.

DINAH (*rising quickly and advancing*). Darling!

BRIAN (*waving her back*). No! No! Stay there! (She retreats and sits at piano.) Go on playing.

(DINAH goes on playing and he takes out a sketch-book, sits on settee and sketches her.)

DINAH. What is it?

(OLIVIA *comes down centre, watching them*.)

BRIAN. Portrait of Lady Strange.

(*GEORGE enters from doors* R. with steps and crossing up R. places them near *R.* window.)

OLIVIA (she hands him the curtains and goes up L. of writing table and round back, watching GEORGE). Are you ready, dear?

GEORGE (*mounting the steps*). Yes, quite ready.

OLIVIA. There! (*The curtains become entangled and he nearly falls*.) Oh, take care, dear!

GEORGE (*again mounting steps*). Oh, that's all right, dear. They're a little long. (*The curtains become entangled round his head*.)

(MR. PIM *enters mysteriously from up* L.)

(OLIVIA *is looking up at* GEORGE.)

(PIM *touches her on the shoulder and with a start she turns to him*. DINAH *seeing him enter stops playing. OLIVIA, unwilling to attract* GEORGE'S *attention, signals to* DINAH to continue playing, and, she does so.)

PIM. Mrs. Marden! I *had* to come back--I've just remembered his name was *Ernest* Polwittle--not *Henry*! (*Going off up* L.) Not Henry!

(DINAH *plays forte*.)

QUICK CURTAIN.

SCENE PLOT

Oak panelled chamber, with deep decorative frieze.

Ceiling cloth, painted with carved oak beams.

Fireplace.--Large open stone fireplace decorated all over with flutings and carved stone

Doors.--Heavy oak doors down R. to open off.

Windows.--C. windows (French windows) opening on stage from terrace.

Stairs.--Stairs up back R. with carved balustrade. Transparent windows stained glass at top of stairway.

Back cloth.--Painted garden and terrace with stone seat C.

PROPERTY PLOT

ACT I

Stage cloth down .--Parquette stage cloth with marble pavement piece attached at back for terrace

Persian carpet laid up and down R.

Persian carpet laid up and down L.

Settee set across down L. (Jacobean settee upholstered in tapestry).

On settee L. Two tapestry cushions.

Occasional Jacobean table to R. of settee down L.

Stool .--Upholstered in rose R. of table.

Semi-grand piano , with keyboard down stage, ***down*** R. below double doors.

On piano .--Dinah's musical instrument.
   Silk pink brocade piano cover.

Photo of Olivia in frame.
Photo of George Marden in frame.
Photo of Dinah in frame.
Photo of Brian in frame.
E.P. mirror.
Blue china bowl containing flowers.
Quantity of music.

Occasional Jacobean chair.--Below piano.

Settee (small Queen Anne cane-backed) upholstered in tapestry set up and down stage against and to L. of piano.

Cushion--dark gold brocade--on settee.

Table (occasional Jacobean) above settee to L., of piano.

On table.--Illustrated papers.
   Rose-coloured piece of brocade.

Chair (occasional Jacobean with rose-coloured squab) L. of occasional table above settee.

Sideboard (Jacobean) up R. against back wall.

On sideboard.--Metal bowl (with flowers)
   Match stand.
   Matches (safety).
   Ash tray.
   Tobacco jar filled.
   George's pipe filled.
   Photo in frame.
   Cigarette box (with cigarettes).

Vase lamp with shade.

Arm-chair (Jacobean with rose-coloured squab)--L. of sideboard
facing out of windows.

Curtains. --Pair of rose-coloured corduroy curtains with tie
backs for centre windows.
Single rose-coloured corduroy curtain for archway up R. hung on upstage
side of arch.

Stairs. --Painted canvas ataircloth.
Brass stair rods.

Occasional chair (Jacobean with rose-coloured squab).--L. of
windows and against back wall.

Table (occasional Jacobean).--Up L. against back wall.
  On table. --Metal bowl containing pink azalea plant in pot.

Writing-table. --In front and below C. windows (leather topped).
  On writing-table. --Specimen glass with flowers
    Writing materials.
    Matches in stand.
    Ash tray.
    Paper and pen rack.
    Small bookcase.

Arm-chair (Jacobean) below writing-table C.

Large cabinet (Jacobean Court cupboard) with three cupboard
doors and on short legs--up L. against L. wall above fireplace.
  In cupboard. --Very pronounced yellow and black

curtains *with webbing arranged* for Olivia to stitch on rings.

Work-box for Olivia containing needles, thread, quantity of rings, scissors.

  On top of cupboard. --Metal bowl with palm in pot.
    Pair of scissors (extra as an emergency for Brian's business).
    Large glass with flowers.

Waste-paper basket. --To L. of writing-table.

Fireplace (L.).--Brass dogs and antique fire tongs.

Combined brass switch and bell pushes on wall down L. below fireplace.

Brass spill-box above bell pushes on wall L. below fireplace.

Table (small Jacobean round cane topped) in angle of fireplace and wall down L. below fireplace.

  On table. --Match stand and matches (safety).
    Ash tray.

Arm-chair (Jacobean with rose-coloured squab) down L. and to R. of circular table L. facing up stage.

Pictures on walls. --Picture in gold frame on wall down R.
  Picture in gold frame on wall above double doors R.
  Picture in gold frame R. of R. wall at back.
  Picture in gold frame L. of R. wall at back.
  Picture in gold frame R. of L. back wall.
  Picture in gold frame L. of L. back wail.

HAND PROPERTIES.

Off R.--Card salver and card for ***Anne***.

Letter in envelope unstamped on salver.

Letter in envelope stamped for Mr. Pim.

Letter in envelope not stamped for ***George Marden***.

Gentleman's visiting card (Mr. Carraway Pim) for George Marden.

ACT II

Same Scene and Properties.
Dinah's small guitar on piano.

Set on Terrace
    3 light green canvas camp chairs.
    2 green and white striped camp chairs.
    Folding camp table with green baize top.

Curtains refolded and placed in cupboard Left.

Off R.
    Large double handled E.P. tray.
    5 coffee cups (coloured for coffee) and saucers
    5 coffee spoons.
    Sugar basin with sugar.

Small hunting crop for *Lady Marden*.
Thick leather gloves for *Lady Marden*.
Cigarette case for *Brian*.

ACT III

Same Set and Furniture as Act II.

Off R.--Pair of short library steps (for *George Marden*).

ELECTRIC PLOT

Chandelier (C.).--Jacobean bronze 6-light chandelier hanging centre NOT lighted.

Brackets on walls.
 One on wall down L.
 One each side of back wall between windows and staircase R.
 One each side of back wall between windows and wall L.
 All above pictures, *not lighted*.

Fire in fireplace, NOT LIGHTED.

Lengths.--Length in stairway, amber and white.
 Length in entrance by double door down R.

Foots.--Amber and white.

Battens.--Ceiling batten, amber and white.
  No. 5 batten, amber and white.

Arcs.--2 perch arcs o.p.)
  2 perch arcs p.s.   ) Light amber and frost.
  No. 1 o.p. flood stage down L.C.
  No. 2 o.p. on settee down R.
  No. 1 p.s. on settee L.
  No. 2 p.s. on stool and flood C.

Flood Arcs.--Two flood arcs on back cloth L. and R.
  Flood arc on transparency windows above stairs R.
  Focus arc through windows C., L. of windows of writing-table
    and doors down R. into room. Sunlight effect.

To open.--All lights full up and remain for Acts I, II and III.

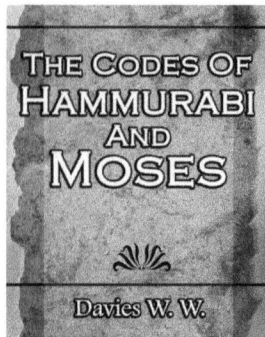

The Codes Of Hammurabi And Moses
W. W. Davies

QTY

The discovery of the Hammurabi Code is one of the greatest achievements of archaeology, and is of paramount interest, not only to the student of the Bible, but also to all those interested in ancient history...

Religion **ISBN:** *1-59462-338-4*

Pages:132

MSRP $12.95

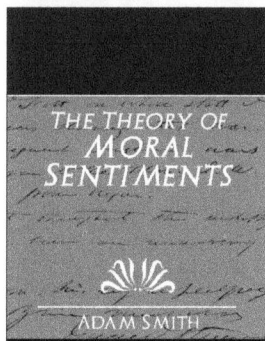

The Theory of Moral Sentiments
Adam Smith

QTY

This work from 1749. contains original theories of conscience amd moral judgment and it is the foundation for systemof morals.

Philosophy **ISBN:** *1-59462-777-0*

Pages:536

MSRP $19.95

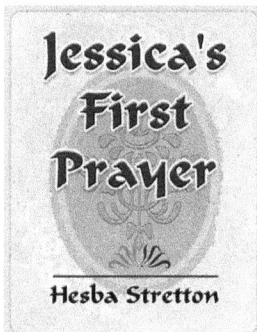

Jessica's First Prayer
Hesba Stretton

QTY

In a screened and secluded corner of one of the many railway-bridges which span the streets of London there could be seen a few years ago, from five o'clock every morning until half past eight, a tidily set-out coffee-stall, consisting of a trestle and board, upon which stood two large tin cans, with a small fire of charcoal burning under each so as to keep the coffee boiling during the early hours of the morning when the work-people were thronging into the city on their way to their daily toil...

Childrens **ISBN:** *1-59462-373-2*

Pages:84

MSRP $9.95

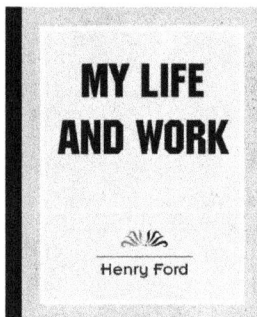

My Life and Work
Henry Ford

QTY

Henry Ford revolutionized the world with his implementation of mass production for the Model T automobile. Gain valuable business insight into his life and work with his own auto-biography... "We have only started on our development of our country we have not as yet, with all our talk of wonderful progress, done more than scratch the surface. The progress has been wonderful enough but..."

Biographies/ **ISBN:** *1-59462-198-5*

Pages:300

MSRP $21.95

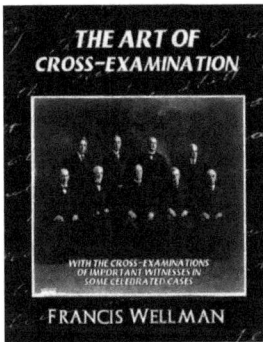

The Art of Cross-Examination
Francis Wellman

QTY

I presume it is the experience of every author, after his first book is published upon an important subject, to be almost overwhelmed with a wealth of ideas and illustrations which could readily have been included in his book, and which to his own mind, at least, seem to make a second edition inevitable. Such certainly was the case with me; and when the first edition had reached its sixth impression in five months, I rejoiced to learn that it seemed to my publishers that the book had met with a sufficiently favorable reception to justify a second and considerably enlarged edition. ..

Reference   ISBN: *1-59462-647-2*

Pages:412

MSRP *$19.95*

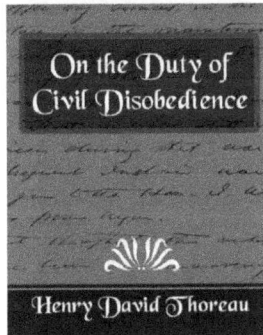

On the Duty of Civil Disobedience
Henry David Thoreau

QTY

Thoreau wrote his famous essay, On the Duty of Civil Disobedience, as a protest against an unjust but popular war and the immoral but popular institution of slave-owning. He did more than write—he declined to pay his taxes, and was hauled off to gaol in consequence. Who can say how much this refusal of his hastened the end of the war and of slavery ?

Law   ISBN: *1-59462-747-9*

Pages:48

MSRP *$7.45*

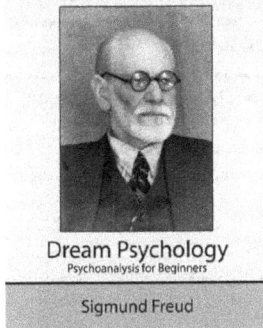

Dream Psychology Psychoanalysis for Beginners
Sigmund Freud

QTY

Sigmund Freud, born Sigismund Schlomo Freud (May 6, 1856 - September 23, 1939), was a Jewish-Austrian neurologist and psychiatrist who co-founded the psychoanalytic school of psychology. Freud is best known for his theories of the unconscious mind, especially involving the mechanism of repression; his redefinition of sexual desire as mobile and directed towards a wide variety of objects; and his therapeutic techniques, especially his understanding of transference in the therapeutic relationship and the presumed value of dreams as sources of insight into unconscious desires.

Psychology   ISBN: *1-59462-905-6*

Pages:196

MSRP *$15.45*

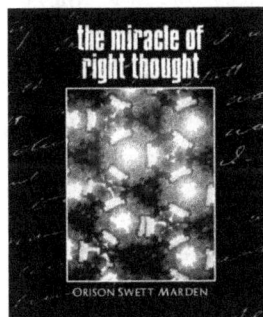

The Miracle of Right Thought
Orison Swett Marden

QTY

Believe with all of your heart that you will do what you were made to do. When the mind has once formed the habit of holding cheerful, happy, prosperous pictures, it will not be easy to form the opposite habit. It does not matter how improbable or how far away this realization may see, or how dark the prospects may be, if we visualize them as best we can, as vividly as possible, hold tenaciously to them and vigorously struggle to attain them, they will gradually become actualized, realized in the life. But a desire, a longing without endeavor, a yearning abandoned or held indifferently will vanish without realization.

Pages:360

Self Help   ISBN: *1-59462-644-8*

MSRP *$25.45*

QTY

The Rosicrucian Cosmo-Conception Mystic Christianity by *Max Heindel* ISBN: *1-59462-188-8* **$38.95**
The Rosicrucian Cosmo-conception is not dogmatic, neither does it appeal to any other authority than the reason of the student. It is: not controversial, but is: sent forth in the, hope that it may help to clear... New Age/Religion Pages 646

Abandonment To Divine Providence by *Jean-Pierre de Caussade* ISBN: *1-59462-228-0* **$25.95**
"The Rev. Jean Pierre de Caussade was one of the most remarkable spiritual writers of the Society of Jesus in France in the 18th Century. His death took place at Toulouse in 1751. His works have gone through many editions and have been republished... Inspirational/Religion Pages 400

Mental Chemistry by *Charles Haanel* ISBN: *1-59462-192-6* **$23.95**
Mental Chemistry allows the change of material conditions by combining and appropriately utilizing the power of the mind. Much like applied chemistry creates something new and unique out of careful combinations of chemicals the mastery of mental chemistry... New Age Pages 354

The Letters of Robert Browning and Elizabeth Barret Barrett 1845-1846 vol II ISBN: *1-59462-193-4* **$35.95**
by *Robert Browning* and *Elizabeth Barrett* Biographies Pages 596

Gleanings In Genesis (volume I) by *Arthur W. Pink* ISBN: *1-59462-130-6* **$27.45**
Appropriately has Genesis been termed "the seed plot of the Bible" for in it we have, in germ form, almost all of the great doctrines which are afterwards fully developed in the books of Scripture which follow... Religion/Inspirational Pages 420

The Master Key by *L. W. de Laurence* ISBN: *1-59462-001-6* **$30.95**
In no branch of human knowledge has there been a more lively increase of the spirit of research during the past few years than in the study of Psychology, Concentration and Mental Discipline. The requests for authentic lessons in Thought Control, Mental Discipline and... New Age/Business Pages 422

The Lesser Key Of Solomon Goetia by *L. W. de Laurence* ISBN: *1-59462-092-X* **$9.95**
This translation of the first book of the "Lernegton" which is now for the first time made accessible to students of Talismanic Magic was done, after careful collation and edition, from numerous Ancient Manuscripts in Hebrew, Latin, and French... New Age/Occult Pages 92

Rubaiyat Of Omar Khayyam by *Edward Fitzgerald* ISBN:*1-59462-332-5* **$13.95**
Edward Fitzgerald, whom the world has already learned, in spite of his own efforts to remain within the shadow of anonymity, to look upon as one of the rarest poets of the century, was born at Bredfield, in Suffolk, on the 31st of March, 1809. He was the third son of John Purcell... Music Pages 172

Ancient Law by *Henry Maine* ISBN: *1-59462-128-4* **$29.95**
The chief object of the following pages is to indicate some of the earliest ideas of mankind, as they are reflected in Ancient Law, and to point out the relation of those ideas to modern thought. Religion/History Pages 452

Far-Away Stories by *William J. Locke* ISBN: *1-59462-129-2* **$19.45**
"Good wine needs no bush, but a collection of mixed vintages does. And this book is just such a collection. Some of the stories I do not want to remain buried for ever in the museum files of dead magazine-numbers an author's not unpardonable vanity..." Fiction Pages 272

Life of David Crockett by *David Crockett* ISBN: *1-59462-250-7* **$27.45**
"Colonel David Crockett was one of the most remarkable men of the times in which he lived. Born in humble life, but gifted with a strong will, an indomitable courage, and unremitting perseverance... Biographies/New Age Pages 424

Lip-Reading by *Edward Nitchie* ISBN: *1-59462-206-X* **$25.95**
Edward B. Nitchie, founder of the New York School for the Hard of Hearing, now the Nitchie School of Lip-Reading, Inc, wrote "LIP-READING Principles and Practice". The development and perfecting of this meritorious work on lip-reading was an undertaking... How-to Pages 400

A Handbook of Suggestive Therapeutics, Applied Hypnotism, Psychic Science ISBN: *1-59462-214-0* **$24.95**
by *Henry Munro* Health/New Age/Health/Self-help Pages 376

A Doll's House: and Two Other Plays by *Henrik Ibsen* ISBN: *1-59462-112-8* **$19.95**
Henrik Ibsen created this classic when in revolutionary 1848 Rome. Introducing some striking concepts in playwriting for the realist genre, this play has been studied the world over. Fiction/Classics/Plays 308

The Light of Asia by *sir Edwin Arnold* ISBN: *1-59462-204-3* **$13.95**
In this poetic masterpiece, Edwin Arnold describes the life and teachings of Buddha. The man who was to become known as Buddha to the world was born as Prince Gautama of India but he rejected the worldly riches and abandoned the reigns of power when... Religion/History/Biographies Pages 170

The Complete Works of Guy de Maupassant by *Guy de Maupassant* ISBN: *1-59462-157-8* **$16.95**
"For days and days, nights and nights, I had dreamed of that first kiss which was to consecrate our engagement, and I knew not on what spot I should put my lips..." Fiction/Classics Pages 240

The Art of Cross-Examination by *Francis L. Wellman* ISBN: *1-59462-309-0* **$26.95**
Written by a renowned trial lawyer, Wellman imparts his experience and uses case studies to explain how to use psychology to extract desired information through questioning. How-to/Science/Reference Pages 408

Answered or Unanswered? by *Louisa Vaughan* ISBN: *1-59462-248-5* **$10.95**
Miracles of Faith in China Religion Pages 112

The Edinburgh Lectures on Mental Science (1909) by *Thomas* ISBN: *1-59462-008-3* **$11.95**
This book contains the substance of a course of lectures recently given by the writer in the Queen Street Hall, Edinburgh. Its purpose is to indicate the Natural Principles governing the relation between Mental Action and Material Conditions... New Age/Psychology Pages 148

Ayesha by *H. Rider Haggard* ISBN: *1-59462-301-5* **$24.95**
Verily and indeed it is the unexpected that happens! Probably if there was one person upon the earth from whom the Editor of this, and of a certain previous history, did not expect to hear again... Classics Pages 380

Ayala's Angel by *Anthony Trollope* ISBN: *1-59462-352-X* **$29.95**
The two girls were both pretty, but Lucy who was twenty-one who supposed to be simple and comparatively unattractive, whereas Ayala was credited, as her Bombwhat romantic name might show, with poetic charm and a taste for romance. Ayala when her father died was nineteen... Fiction Pages 484

The American Commonwealth by *James Bryce* ISBN: *1-59462-286-8* **$34.45**
An interpretation of American democratic political theory. It examines political mechanics and society from the perspective of Scotsman James Bryce Politics Pages 572

Stories of the Pilgrims by *Margaret P. Pumphrey* ISBN: *1-59462-116-0* **$17.95**
This book explores pilgrims religious oppression in England as well as their escape to Holland and eventual crossing to America on the Mayflower, and their early days in New England... History Pages 268

www.bookjungle.com *email: sales@bookjungle.com fax: 630-214-0564 mail: Book Jungle PO Box 2226 Champaign, IL 61825*

QTY

The Fasting Cure *by Sinclair Upton*   ISBN: *1-59462-222-1*   **$13.95**
*In the Cosmopolitan Magazine for May, 1910, and in the Contemporary Review (London) for April, 1910, I published an article dealing with my experi-
ences in fasting. I have written a great many magazine articles, but never one which attracted so much attention...* New Age/Self Help/Health Pages 164

Hebrew Astrology *by Sepharial*   ISBN: *1-59462-308-2*   **$13.45**
*In these days of advanced thinking it is a matter of common observation that we have left many of the old landmarks behind and that we are now pressing
forward to greater heights and to a wider horizon than that which represented the mind-content of our progenitors...* Astrology Pages 144

Thought Vibration or The Law of Attraction in the Thought World   ISBN: *1-59462-127-6*   **$12.95**

by William Walker Atkinson   Psychology/Religion Pages 144

Optimism *by Helen Keller*   ISBN: *1-59462-108-X*   **$15.95**
*Helen Keller was blind, deaf, and mute since 19 months old, yet famously learned how to overcome these handicaps, communicate with the world, and
spread her lectures promoting optimism. An inspiring read for everyone...* Biographies/Inspirational Pages 84

Sara Crewe *by Frances Burnett*   ISBN: *1-59462-360-0*   **$9.45**
*In the first place, Miss Minchin lived in London. Her home was a large, dull, tall one, in a large, dull square, where all the houses were alike, and all the
sparrows were alike, and where all the door-knockers made the same heavy sound...* Childrens/Classic Pages 88

The Autobiography of Benjamin Franklin *by Benjamin Franklin*   ISBN: *1-59462-135-7*   **$24.95**
*The Autobiography of Benjamin Franklin has probably been more extensively read than any other American historical work, and no other book of its kind
has had such ups and downs of fortune. Franklin lived for many years in England, where he was agent...* Biographies/History Pages 332

Name	
Email	
Telephone	
Address	
City, State ZIP	

☐ **Credit Card**   ☐ **Check / Money Order**

Credit Card Number	
Expiration Date	
Signature	

*Please Mail to: Book Jungle
PO Box 2226
Champaign, IL 61825
or Fax to: 630-214-0564*

ORDERING INFORMATION

web: *www.bookjungle.com*
email: *sales@bookjungle.com*
fax: *630-214-0564*
mail: *Book Jungle PO Box 2226 Champaign, IL 61825*
or PayPal *to sales@bookjungle.com*

Please contact us for bulk discounts

DIRECT-ORDER TERMS

**20% Discount if You Order
Two or More Books**
Free Domestic Shipping!
Accepted: Master Card, Visa,
Discover, American Express

www.ingramcontent.com/pod-product-compliance
Lightning Source LLC
Chambersburg PA
CBHW081233090426
42738CB00016B/3293